The Value Proposition Matrix

An Innovator's Guide
to Four Questions That
Separate Success from Failure

By

Brandon R. Cornuke

Library of Congress Control Number: 2022905592

ISBN: 979-8-9860168-0-1

Book design by Ben Small, Live Publishing Co.

To Whitney, Tessa, Eloise, and Sadie.
You are my greatest project, my inspiration,
my compass, my purpose.

Contents

Foreword vii

Preface 1

Chapter One
Harnessing the Gale of Creative Destruction................. 5

Chapter Two
Know Your Value 21

Chapter Three
What You Know for Sure that Just Ain't So................. 50

Chapter Four
Vetting Demand 67

Chapter Five
Vetting Supply 95

Chapter Six
Bringing it Together..120

Chapter Seven
Biases..128

Chapter Eight
The Winding Road to Success 138

Appendix...143

Endnotes 148

Foreword

By Ethan Karp, Ph.D.

When I was four years old, I decided to build what I thought would be a better mousetrap. I made a box out of plastic, construction paper, and masking tape. Then I put coins inside to lure the unsuspecting mouse. It never trapped a mouse, and there's no way it ever could. But I keep it on my desk to remind me of my passion for making things. And trying to make them better. If you share this same passion, this book is for you.

The Value Proposition Matrix is a practical guide to help you turn your ideas into winning innovations. Because let's face it, having an idea is the easy part. Turning that idea into a product that people buy and a company that makes money — that's a much tougher proposition. This book's author, Brandon Cornuke, and I know this firsthand. At our non-profit organization, MAGNET: The Manufacturing Advocacy & Growth Network, we've helped thousands of entrepreneurs and start-ups navigate the relentless ups and downs of innovation.

Today's start-up world is software and technology dominated and Silicon Valley obsessed. But we have a different focus. We help would-be manufacturers in Ohio invent real, physical products. Innovation is always challenging but this is a particularly difficult space to succeed in. We see start-up manufacturers crashing into obstacles all the time: a dearth of investors, difficulty finding space and talent, and razor-thin margins for error.

There is always more risk with manufactured products versus virtual ones. Prototyping and testing real products is expensive, time-consuming, and sometimes even dangerous. There are not a lot of investors willing to throw capital at startups that need to buy raw materials and equipment, establish supply chains, train employees, and lease factory space.

But physical product entrepreneurs persevere because we all recognize that the manufacturing industry desperately needs fresh, technology-driven upstarts. Manufacturing growth will only come through innovation. Without it, the industry will inevitably shrink. The reality is, there is no American manufacturing revival without innovation. We can't lead the world if we're standing still. Our future is not incremental. It's big, bold ideas that bring smart manufacturing to life by infusing digital, connected technology into products that people use every day. This means we need more innovation across the board — from big companies, small companies, spinoffs, and startups. But unfortunately, that's not happening. We recently surveyed hundreds of manufacturers in Northeast Ohio and 75% said that innovation is not a top priority for them.

I completely understand why. Innovation seems risky, scary, and expensive. But the solution is not to avoid it. In the midwest heartland of manufacturing, we must overcome our innate conservatism and rethink our entire approach to risk. We need to de-risk the process of invention and innovation. And that's what this book sets out to do.

The ideas and approaches that Brandon guides us through have been road tested by MAGNET's team with thousands of entrepreneurs and start-ups. I've been privileged to be in the trenches with Brandon and his start-up experts for the past eight years. We're a non-profit consultancy, so we're able to help small and mid-sized manufacturers and start-ups who can't afford the higher fees of traditional consultants. We've had our expected (luckily small) share of failures and flops, but many more amazing successes. Like a company that builds robots that can teach themselves how to weld (and has raised over $170 million). An automated sewing startup that produced more than ten million masks for the state of Ohio during the COVID-19 pandemic. And an entrepreneur who invented a power system that exponentially increases the range of drones. We've not only helped these start-ups, we've also learned from them. And their stories and insights shaped the Value Proposition Matrix.

The heart of getting innovation right is asking the right questions, four of them to be exact: Are you solving a real problem? Does your product actually solve the problem? Are you the right person to deliver this solution? And can you sell it? Consider my childhood mousetrap. We had no problem with rodents in my house. My invention didn't actually work. I had no ability to improve on my design. And being four, I had no ability to sell it. Thankfully, I didn't need the Value Proposition Matrix to tell me to abandon my idea — I simply moved on the next shiny object. But you'd be surprised how many entrepreneurs get far down the start-up road without asking and systematically answering these questions. When startups fail, nearly half the time it's because they offer something the market doesn't need in the first place.

As Thomas Edison said, "There's a way to do it better. Find it." This book will help you do innovation better — whether you're a start-up, a serial entrepreneur, an intrapreneur inside an established company, or simply a person with an idea. It's an easy read full of great stories and advice. And Brandon is exactly the right person to lead you through this journey. Yes, he has deep expertise and all the right things on his resume: Vice President of Strategy and Innovation at MAGNET, Adjunct Professor of Design and Innovation at the Weatherhead School of Management at Case Western Reserve University in Cleveland, and he's a start-up founder himself. But beyond all this, Brandon has something even more important: passion. He is a quintessential innovator. He lives and breathes it. He has a constant fire in his belly to help people bring their ideas to life. Innovation is his life's work and that shines through in his writing, his commitment to the manufacturing start-up community, and his deep belief that we need to support and nurture new inventions that make people's lives better.

When Brandon first came to me with the idea to write this book, I loved it. But it gave me pause. I couldn't see how he could possibly find the time to write with his full-time job at MAGNET, his teaching, his own company, and a young family. But against all odds, including a global pandemic, he made time and he made it happen. Brandon — it's a true honor to work with you and I look forward to seeing how your ideas continue to inspire and help your fellow innovators and the manufacturing industry. I also want to thank the rest of the start-up team at MAGNET who work tirelessly to help manufacturing start-ups take root and grow. Your work shaped the ideas in this book, and you should be very proud. And, of course, none of this work would be possible without the funders and tireless partners we are so grateful for: NIST-MEP, Ohio MEP, Third Frontier, and the Entrepreneurial Services Programs of the Ohio Department of Development.

As this book goes to press, the world is emerging from a global pandemic. It's been a tumultuous two years, but now is exactly the right time to start thinking about doing more innovation and doing it faster and better. After every global crisis there's a spike in innovation, start-ups, and patent filings. The Great Depression gave us the photocopier and the Polaroid camera. The SARS outbreak helped Alibaba become an e-commerce giant. The global financial crisis created Airbnb. We're living through massive shifts in consumer behavior and there will be a huge wave of post-pandemic innovation. A wave the manufacturing industry can ride to growth — if we ask ourselves the right (four) questions and use the answers to make smart bets on innovation.

Dr. Ethan Karp is the President and CEO of MAGNET, Northeast Ohio's preeminent center for manufacturing talent, transformation, and innovation. Ethan has a Ph.D. in Chemical

Biology from Harvard University, is a former consultant with McKinsey & Company, and is a regular contributor for Forbes. His columns have been featured on Fast Company, Crain's, and Industry Week.

The Value Proposition Matrix™

Preface

"As a startup CEO, I slept like a baby.
I woke up every two hours and cried."

— Ben Horowitz, Venture Capitalist and Co-Founder,
Andreessen Horowitz

As the old saying goes, "Entrepreneurs don't really own their startups; their startups own them." The same is true for innovators inside companies, where bringing ideas to life can be just as grueling. Commercial innovation in any form requires tireless dedication and a unique combination of guts, brains, and luck.

Today, starting a company, launching a new product, or developing a new business model is more complicated than ever. Technology has rearranged nearly every aspect of our lives, creating massive shifts in the competitive landscape. Big firms are consolidating at record rates. Globalization is coalescing a network of disparate markets and supply chains, while a pandemic is rearranging them. Government regulations, trade rules, and tax codes grow more inscrutable every year. Intellectual property thieves and patent trolls terrorize the well-prepared and unprepared alike. Google, Facebook, and Amazon have fundamentally altered the way we market every imaginable product. We work, eat, learn, play, travel, buy, sell, connect, and communicate in ways that have been forever altered by computer processors and strings of code.

It's a thrilling time to be a consumer. But to the innovator trying to launch a new product or service, it can feel hopelessly overwhelming. Because I've spent much of my career helping innovators and starting my own ventures, I've experienced these struggles firsthand.

I've found that early-stage innovators — those whose ideas are just taking shape — encounter several common, yet potentially ruinous, issues. They can't explain the essential elements of their ideas, or how those pieces fit together to create value; nor can they articulate which fundamental assumptions they're making, much less how they plan to vet those assumptions.

But these impediments rarely reflect flaws in the idea itself. In my experience, many innovators simply need better tools to help them hone their thinking, illuminate the most likely hazards, and streamline the journey from idea to launch and beyond.

Bookstores are thick with guides and frameworks meant to do just that. But while I've read, referenced, and recombined many of these over the years, I have yet to find one that crisply and concisely helps innovators clarify a business idea, identify their fundamental assumptions, and navigate their biggest unknowns.

Over time, I developed a toolset that I came to call the Value Proposition Matrix. As I shared my approach, my clients and students consistently asked for more context and content. That's how this book began to take shape — it is my attempt to cut through the confusion that stymies innovators.

I've often heard the complaint — and occasionally agreed — that most business books could be articles instead. I don't want to fall into the same trap here, so I'll summarize what you'll find expanded in the following chapters.

Business ideas are built on four elements: a customer, their problem, a solution, and the team to deliver it. No matter the configuration of these four elements, they rest on four assumptions: that the problem is important, that the solution solves the problem, that the team can deliver the solution, and the customer will buy it. Identifying these four elements and finding the assumptions that are most likely to be wrong is the key to successful innovation.

That's it. If you prefer your books in article form — or, in this case, a paragraph — my work is done. However, if you want to better understand these four elements and the assumptions that lurk within, I invite you to read on.

Make no mistake; creating new businesses will always be devilishly hard, but it doesn't have to be quite so confounding. The Value Proposition Matrix is a simple toolkit to help illuminate the initial steps of that journey and strip away some of the complexity.

In this book, I'll walk you through the four core value questions that will help you build a rock-solid value proposition. I'll also explain how to uncover those lurking assumptions and show you how to vet them in the marketplace — all to give your idea the best chance of success. Whether you're creating a startup from scratch or launching a new business model inside a company, these tools will help you become a more efficient, resilient innovator.

The stories I reference are true and come from personal experiences. But to respect the anonymity of my clients, students, and colleagues and maintain appropriate confidentiality, I have changed names and non-material details where appropriate. Also, while I could draw on experiences in a broad range of industries and technologies, from robotics and machine learning to financial software and e-commerce, I've deliberately chosen to use straightforward examples that offer the most widely accessible insights. Hopefully, this approach helps better illuminate the ideas in this book. I have also included a short synopsis before each chapter to make it easy to reference the important themes.

While a framework will never replace a great idea, hustle, and plenty of good fortune, my goal in sharing these concepts is to help you put your time and energy to good use, improving your chances of success.

Innovators are some of the most inspiring people I know. They're often courageous and optimistic, and they usually want to make the world a better place. Making that path a little easier and sparking more successes has been gratifying beyond measure. Thanks for letting me join you on your innovation journey.

Chapter One
Harnessing the Gale of Creative Destruction

Synopsis: To keep up with the dramatic acceleration in innovation, startups and established companies alike have begun looking for faster, more efficient ways to start new ventures. But the available tools don't do a good job helping innovators articulate their value proposition and their assumptions. It's difficult to succeed without a firm understanding of both.

1.1 The Old Ways vs. The New Wave

"The gale of creative destruction incessantly revolutionizes the economic structure within, incessantly destroying the old one, incessantly creating the new one."

— Joseph Schumpeter, Harvard University Economist

Imagine it's 1959, and you are the CEO of one of the 500 largest companies in the United States. You're the captain of a hulking organization, and you oversee a corporate empire that's sailing through one of the greatest periods of economic expansion in history. Your company's prospects look just as promising as the economic boom unfolding around you. At the time, the average

Fortune 500 Company could expect to stay on that prestigious list for more than six decades.

If, instead, you were a Fortune 500 CEO in 2021, you wouldn't be nearly as confident — and for good reason. Newer Fortune 500 firms have shown far less staying power, just 16 years. One big reason? Waves of innovation are capsizing large companies just as quickly as they overwhelm upstarts. This is what the economist Joseph Schumpeter called creative destruction — now commonly referred to as disruption — and it's currently raging with a building intensity. Today's CEOs don't just have to fret about other behemoth competitors, they are equally right to worry about an obscure startup making their $100 million product line obsolete, seemingly overnight.

Technology has continued to fuel a growing hurricane of innovation. As I write this, the average smartphone has a thousand times more computing power than the Apollo 11 spacecraft that landed on the moon. Robots and algorithms are doing more work, more efficiently than armies of human beings ever could. Autonomous vehicles promise to transform the way we move goods and people, revolutionizing supply chains and urban plans. Communication systems and social media platforms connect people and experiences across the globe, spreading ideas and sparking trends at an astonishing rate. Augmented and virtual reality programs are changing the way we visualize our world, allowing architects to walk through buildings before they've been built and doctors to see complex neural structures for the first time. Medical breakthroughs extend our lives, leading some experts to predict a future in which we might even forestall old age entirely.

As this cycle of creative destruction accelerates, a new "lean" way of thinking about innovation has emerged.

In a business context, thinking lean means eliminating wasted effort and money through inexpensive experimentation and rapid adjustments. To lean innovators, the ways organizations have traditionally tried to innovate are wasteful. Here's a summary of the old method:

1. Come up with a new product idea.
2. Use consultants and focus groups to assess whether enough customers want it.
3. Raise (or allocate) as much money as possible to support production and marketing.
4. Build the necessary supply chain as efficiently as possible.
5. Launch in familiar channels with lots of advertising or sales support.
6. Hope for the best.

Business executives and managers taking this approach presume that with enough research and preparation, sales will mushroom and profits will pile up. Of course, for that to happen, the product, price, promotional strategy, and distribution must be just right. And the competition must be far enough behind. Failure is measured in millions of dollars, and the blame falls on anyone associated with the project. Even in success, innovators generally make big, costly miscalculations and bad design decisions. Giving up on failed product development is even more difficult. Business leaders often fear the stain of failure or clutch onto their ideas with conviction.

But startups and large companies alike have begun to realize that this "build it and they will come" paradigm can be massively improved. A revolutionary suite of tools and techniques is helping them bend the blistering rate of change to their advantage.

Concepts like Lean Startup, Agile software development, Design Thinking, and Customer Discovery have all been built on the insight that smaller, faster, iterative steps are far more effective and efficient than big, linear processes and projects. At the same time, the Internet, combined with advances in design techniques, software engineering, 3D printing, and digital marketing tools, have made quick experimentation practical and effective.

Practitioners of these new methods use simple design tools and iterative experimentation, enabling them to try something new and learn efficiently without over-investing. This method quickly and inexpensively generates loads of insights and sharpens unrefined ideas. Testing the best of those ideas creates new or improved products. Measuring how those products perform creates data, which, in turn, drives more learning.

In his book, *The Lean Startup* (2011), Eric Ries calls this the Build-Measure-Learn cycle. Rather than trying to create the perfect product from the get-go, a growing number of companies see the wisdom in creating *imperfect* products and improving (or killing) them as quickly as possible. This cycle replaces guesses with evidence, which improves the likelihood of success. Evidence-based entrepreneurship replaces instinct and assumptions with experimentation and fact-gathering.

Countless startups have used these techniques to avoid wasting money and time on ideas that customers wouldn't buy, which has led to winning business ideas like Zappos, Dropbox, and Dollar Shave Club. Likewise, large companies have used these tools to create both incremental and breakthrough innovations. For example:

- In hotels around the world, Marriott chose small teams of employees and local entrepreneurs to experiment with new food and beverage service concepts. Creators of the winning concepts got up to $50,000 and six months to turn their visions into reality.
- Google Ventures has developed a five-day process for answering critical business questions through a rapid-fire process of designing, prototyping, and testing ideas with customers.

- Lego's Futures Lab team handmade 200 sets to test whether consumers would buy Lego building replicas. They sold these sets through specialty retailers in the Chicago area at twice the average retail price, providing quick validation for what would become the hugely popular Architecture series.
- Even the government has joined the lean revolution. A Defense Department-sponsored lean startup initiative is developing technologies and deploying them faster in response to "security threats."

While lean frameworks are changing the way many organizations innovate, rapid design and experimentation take patience, trust, and experience. Books like *The Lean Startup, The Business Model Canvas* (2008), *The Startup Owner's Manual* (2012), *Value Proposition Design* (2014), *Talking to Humans* (2014), *and Sprint* (2016), have built and expanded on an impressive array of tools. But the broader lean innovation playbook is still missing a chapter on how to simplify early-stage idea exploration.

Most early-innovators can better organize and prioritize their first steps. I've seen these issues plague innovators in the classroom and across a wide spectrum of organizations, including seedling startups, large companies, nonprofits, professional sports teams, hospital systems, and cultural institutions.

As an entrepreneur, I am certainly not immune to these challenges. I dealt with the same struggles when I co-founded a spray-on body powder company called Dry Goods.

1.2 Dry Goods

When Tim Joyce and I met at Northwestern's Kellogg School of Management, we instantly bonded over our shared ambition to start a business. This was as much a product of our personalities as it was about the economy at the time. It was the fall of 2008 and, from the cozy confines of our full-time MBA program, we had front row seats to the global financial meltdown. What would later be called the Great Recession had just toppled Bear Stearns and Lehman Brothers. Classmates hoping to join the Wall Street bonanza met a jarringly barren recruiting cycle, and we all quickly faced the gloom of a crumbling job market. Companies in every industry were slowing or freezing their hiring processes. We had applied to MBA programs when the market was sizzling, but in the months between receiving our acceptance letters and arriving for the first day of classes, our zeal had all but evaporated.

Against this backdrop, Tim and I thought entrepreneurship sounded more fun and potentially more fruitful than job hunting. But we had no idea what kind of company to start. So, we began batting around ideas focused on the problems we found in everyday life. One night over beers (naturally), one of us mentioned body powders — the talcy white substance people dump on their skin (usually, in their underwear) to keep dry and reduce friction. "Yeah, that stuff is messy," Tim said, "but the guys who use it swear by it." I had a similar impression. Body powder was handy, but did it need to be so messy? How big was that market anyway?

The answer surprised us. At the time, body powder was worth over $150 million in the US and far more globally. Big brands like Gold Bond and Johnson's Baby Powder dominated the category, with more than 50% market share. Body powders could be found in every big box retailer, grocery chain, and drug store.

Given its size, we were puzzled by the lack of innovation in the category. Other skincare products like deodorants, lotions, and shaving creams had all undergone major improvements over the last several decades, from formulation to packaging. As far as we could tell, body powders hadn't changed much in a hundred years. Customers using the product in 1908 would've had nearly the exact same user experience as those using it in 2008.

Through our informal research, Tim and I learned something else. When we asked our friends about the product, those who used it were seriously passionate about it. Body powder users weren't mere consumers; they were enthusiasts. We were sold. This was the problem we wanted to solve. We spent the next 18 months building a new body powder brand based on the problem at the heart of our original hypothesis: dump-on powders were messy. We called the project Dry Goods.

We began by talking to powder users and using it ourselves. Then we started trying to come up with unique solutions. We thought of creams that dried or powders that could be rolled on like deodorant. We even considered a permeable bag that could be used to powder those tender parts. We looked at the way other dusty, chalky products were applied to the skin, like chalk bags.

Finally, Tim and I decided on an aerosol application. An aerosol can would be a familiar product in the bathroom or gym, but we also believed it would solve the mess problem.

Since neither of us had experience with formulations, we needed a chemist. We also had no way to mass-produce sprayable, skin-safe powder and package it in an aerosol container. An East Coast manufacturer solved both problems when they offered to help us develop the chemistry and the delivery mechanism for a fee. In return, we agreed to work with them to make and fulfill the final product.

After several months of development — and a few hilarious rounds of testing — we found a great formula (speaking from painful experience, be careful with the amount of menthol you add to products that will be applied to sensitive parts of the body). Our product could be sprayed on in a liquid layer, where it would instantly dry into an even coat of soft, white powder. It stayed where you sprayed it, and it dramatically reduced the amount of powder that landed on clothing or the floor.

With some money from friends and family and funds from

a pitch competition we'd won, we paid for our first production run of more than 30,000 units. We had our inventory shipped to a third-party logistics partner who waited to ship crates to retailers as we made the sales that we were completely confident would come.

But as time passed, I came to realize that our confidence in the demand for our product — and our laser focus on supply — was a mistake. Aside from a few online retail channels, brick-and-mortar stores were largely unwilling to make orders.

Two things stood in the way: first, they asked to see our sales data because they wanted evidence that consumers would buy the product before they'd stock it. Second, retailers didn't understand where to place our product. Should it go with the spray-on underarm deodorants? How about near the foot sprays? Even putting it next to the body powders was complicated because no two retailers stock body powders in the same location. Body powder might fall under the foot care buyer (one of the people responsible for choosing what goes on the shelves) at one drug store chain and under the men's personal care buyer at another. In other words, the retail dynamics sideswiped us. Grinding out every sale, we landed some small retail accounts, but getting the wholesale channel running was a brutally slow process.

In the meantime, we attracted the attention of the big body powder players. Just 18 months after Dry Goods launched, Chattem, the company that owns Gold Bond, launched an aerosol version of its signature product. There was little doubt that our project had thrown our competition into action. We watched as their product outcompeted us for retail space and, thanks to their production scale advantages, beat us on price. They had one other unassailable advantage: name recognition. The Gold Bond logo on an aerosol can instantly makes sense to consumers. Dry Goods had to work much harder to communicate its value proposition.

The Dry Goods brand never realized the scope and scale

Tim and I hoped it would. As the world's first spray-on body powder, we created a new product sub-category — one that can now be found on retail shelves around the world. But in entrepreneurship, moral victories don't count, and seeing the success of the concept is equal parts gratifying and painful.

But that experience — however painful — also ignited my fascination with innovation and a deep desire to turn ideas into successful businesses. Because of my own bruising defeat, I was able to develop the tools that form the foundation of this book. For example, I will introduce the framework using one of the fundamental challenges we faced when trying to build Dry Goods: explaining the value of our product to retailers. After all, retailers are the gateway to consumers.

1.3 Best Laid Plans?

No matter the environment, succinctly describing the essence and value of an idea is often a difficult process. There are common ways to approach this problem, and I get to see these each time I sit down with a new innovator. They might produce a drawing on a napkin, or a hundred-page business plan. If they're familiar with lean innovation, they might share a business model. Let's briefly explore each.

The Sketch

Most of the time, innovators offer a brief description (often quite literally a drawing) along with stories about how they came up with the idea, how they've been thinking about it for a long time, and how much their friends and family love it. This explanation often follows three steps. First come details about the product or service, including how it will be made or delivered. Next come the confident assurances that it will sell. Finally, of course, we arrive at the certainty of profits. I see this pattern so frequently that I call it the "Build-Sell-Profit" model (see Figure 1).

Figure 1

While I appreciate that they haven't over-invested in developing their ideas, these entrepreneurs usually struggle to concisely explain how they plan to create value and for whom. ("It's for everyone!") If I don't guide the conversation, it's typical to spend half an hour wandering before we can gather their thoughts into something concrete and cohesive.

The Business Plan

On the other hand, an entrepreneur might bring me a traditional business plan — complete with chapters, colorful charts, and the heft to make it look thorough. Unfortunately, the amount of preparation that goes into creating a weighty tome doesn't automatically make it easier to understand. All that writing generally has the opposite effect. Mountains of text often mask murky thinking and wild guesses.

The Business Model

Occasionally an entrepreneur brings me a business model — typically a single page with several connected elements that explain how they think they'll be able to make money with a new idea. The most common frameworks are the Business Model Canvas (Osterwalder) and the Lean Canvas (Maurya).

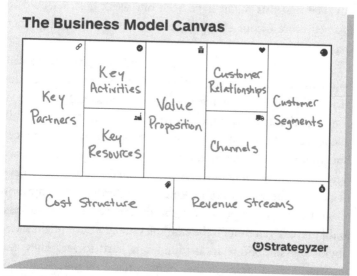

The Business Model Canvas (Strategyzer.com)

Osterwalder's canvas — built on nine questions — can help entrepreneurs explain important concepts like value propositions and target customers.

I vastly prefer a canvas to a sketch or a business plan. Osterwalder and his collaborators have helped countless innovators distill their business models into essential pieces. However, these tools also push early innovators to contemplate questions that can (and probably should) be addressed much later. For instance, I can't tell you how many times I've had innovators come to me in a panic about sorting out their distribution channels or revenue models before they've sold a single product.

More importantly, I've found precious few examples where an entrepreneur has used these tools to quickly identify their most important assumptions — the critical elements of an idea that require the most guesswork. For example, while developing Dry Goods, we missed a lot of assumptions about the way retailers and consumers understood our product — a crucial prerequisite for anyone making a purchase. Understanding in advance that this might have been our weak link, I would've focused more of our efforts on early sales experiments rather than shoring up supply.

Assumptions come in all shapes and sizes, and some can be far more important than others. Whether anyone needs the product or service is a big one. According to CB Insights, a company that tracks technology trends, 35% of all startups fail due to a simple lack of market need for their product or service. But aiming marketing at the wrong customer can be just as fatal for a burgeoning business with limited funds. This is key: **as an innovator, you are making several critical assumptions — and these assumptions are the difference between success and failure.** Even though the examples noted above might seem obvious, assumptions are astoundingly hard to see. They are the invisible elephants in the room, often only understood in the bright light of hindsight.

Identifying and testing your critical assumptions allows you to prioritize resources and make meaningful progress, rather than spending a lot of time and money on an idea that has a catastrophic flaw.

1.4 Why Assumptions Matter

It's reasonable to question whether all this talk about finding assumptions matters in the real world. Frameworks can over-promise on benefits and under-deliver on results. However, it may be useful to illustrate the power of assumptions through a story.

Bob Winskowicz and Robb Osinski are the founders of Performance Indicators, LLC. Their company developed a concept that they believed could double or triple the size of the golf ball market. Bob and Robb knew that the performance of golf balls that had been submerged in water for days or weeks would eventually degrade. They also knew that hundreds of thousands of golf balls were pulled out of golf course ponds and waterways every year, and that the average golfer played with two used balls for every new ball they purchased. That meant thousands of golfers were playing with compromised equipment and that golf ball manufacturers — whose market is projected to surpass $1.3 Billion by 2025 — were potentially missing out on hundreds of millions of dollars in new sales each year. If you aren't a golfer, these might not seem like serious issues; how much could a little ball cost? In 2021, the top-selling golf ball in the world, the Titleist ProV1, made and distributed by Acushnet — retails for $49.99 per dozen, or $4.16 *per ball*.

Along with a team of chemists, Bob and Robb set out to solve this problem by developing a chemical coating that would change color when exposed to water for a certain length of time. Imagine a vividly white golf ball that, after spending a few weeks submerged in water, gradually turned an ashen gray. The golfer who fishes this gray ball out of the water would know that it was unusable and toss it, likely opting to buy a new ball instead. Likewise, professionals who collect and resell lost golf balls would know when one of their finds was unusable. That, too, would put more new balls into circulation.

Bob and Robb surmised that if manufacturers began coating golf balls with the Performance Indicator chemical compound, it would unlock hundreds of millions of dollars of value and improve the playing experience for golfers everywhere. After five years of investment and development, Bob and Robb landed on just the right formulation and were ready to present it to manufacturers.

With a valuable idea like that, their success was all but assured, right? Let's uncover some of the assumptions Bob and Robb were making.

Who did Bob and Robb imagine would benefit from Performance Indicator? First, manufacturers would reap millions in additional sales if water-damaged balls were taken out of circulation each year. But, of course, licensing or buying the proprietary chemistry and adding it to their golf balls would cost money.

Thus, a manufacturer would have to believe their sales would go up enough to offset that cost or that they could pass the additional cost onto customers. Following that logic, would a customer pay extra for Performance Indicator? Not likely, because they wouldn't benefit from the additional investment. The person who finds their lost ball will. In other words, the value funded by one consumer accrues to someone else. Worse, that "someone else" benefits by knowing whether to play or discard the ball they acquired for the negligible cost of picking it up. Known as a "free-rider" problem, this dynamic makes it highly unlikely that consumers would bear any additional cost — in fact, they might prefer not to buy Performance Indicator golf balls, hoping that someone else doesn't benefit from their costly purchase.

Likewise, manufacturers would face a similar free-rider problem. If Acushnet, for example, were to add Performance Indicator to its ProV1 balls, anyone who found the ball would benefit. But that lucky golfer wouldn't necessarily buy Achushnet's balls after discovering a compromised ProV1 ball. They would be just as likely to buy a new ball from any one of Acushnet's competitors.

In this context, it's easier to spot the suspect assumption that Bob and Robb made. They believed their customers (manufacturers) and end consumers (golfers) would see the overall value Performance Indicator could generate for the market. However, that value would not necessarily accrue to the golfer or to the manufacturer who paid for the technology. Bob and Robb made a guess about the market and launched head-first into developing and perfecting their product without exploring their initial assumptions.

I cannot overstate how important it is for innovators to identify critical assumptions and test them as quickly as possible. Bob and Robb spent years and a lot of money building something that consumers ultimately didn't want. Imagine all the time and money they could have saved had they first opted to focus on talking to customers.

But before we're too critical of Bob and Robb, we should acknowledge that **figuring out which assumptions matter most isn't easy, especially at the beginning of a project.**

Bob and Robb made hundreds of assumptions the minute they sketched out their initial idea. But it bears repeating; isolating the most critical assumptions is difficult, especially when you're close to a project. The details we think are important, like, "Can I get the chemistry to react to water in exactly the right way?" overshadow the bigger picture questions, like, "Am I creating value for the right consumer?"

Isolating the assumptions that matter separates innovators who use their scarce resources wisely from those who squander them.

The first step to finding critical assumptions, most guides suggest, is to list them. Inevitably, this produces a long list of unknowns, some important, some less so. What price should I charge? Which customers should I focus on? How durable, fast, precise, light, reliable, or disposable should the product be? Should I sell through wholesale, retail, or direct-to-consumer channels? These questions go on endlessly, and the more complex the model, the more assumptions emerge. Coming up with all the assumptions that underpin a bulky business plan, for example, is like asking someone to count all the bricks at Wrigley Field. It's a daunting process. And the basic napkin sketch of an idea contains just as many — if not more — assumptions.

That's where many of the single-sheet business model tools are supposed to come in. Breaking down a business idea into, say, nine interconnected questions is meant to add color and structure to the napkin sketch while streamlining the business plan. In theory, this is a sound approach, but it doesn't always work in practice. It is still difficult to pull the most critical assumptions out of the typical one-sheet canvas, and it often leads to lists and lists of unknowns. That's a headache, even for those who do have time and experience.

After trying these tools again and again, I was able to pinpoint those assumptions that were most critical to success. I'll share those with you in Chapter Three.

First, I want to cover the first step in finding assumptions — developing a sound value proposition. Whether they have a sketch, a business plan, a business model, or a combination of all three, innovators regularly struggle to articulate how they plan to create value for consumers. Incorrect assumptions can derail the best laid plans but when innovators misunderstand and miscommunicate the value they hope to create, they risk missing their assumptions entirely. There's a better way.

Chapter Two
Know Your Value

Synopsis: Innovators can boil their ideas down to an essential value proposition by asking four questions:

- Who will be our first customer?
- What problem are we solving?
- What unique product are we offering?
- What special assets does our team have?

2.1 Coming in Clear

"Always the beautiful answer who asks a more beautiful question."
— E. E. Cummings

When I met Terrance, his company had already been recycling industrial byproducts (mostly metals) for more than two decades. He and his small team reached out to my team at MAG-NET, a Northeast Ohio non-profit consulting firm that supports manufacturers and product startups, for help developing a machine that he hoped would allow his company to enter a new market. When Terrance, his partner Joe, and my team met in my office, I asked them to tell me about their project. They reached for a laptop, propped their screen in my direction, and began flipping through roughly 50 PowerPoint slides. After 45 minutes, they'd explained in detail the science, supply chain, and economics behind a complex process. As far as I could tell, it used a combination of chemical engineering and licensed military technology to make something that both Terrance and Joe thought was very important. My team and I, however, were baffled. They had just hit us with an avalanche of information. It was far too much to process.

Terrence, for all his knowledge and experience, had not developed a clear value proposition. **While the term "value proposition" is used in many ways, I define it as the offer a company makes to consumers that sets it apart from its competition.** I couldn't find that information in what they'd told me, at least not in a way that I could explain it to someone else.

The next day I met another entrepreneur over eggs and coffee. "Have you tried to buy a mailbox lately?" Dwight asked, his enthusiasm creating a delightfully unexpected contrast with his subject matter. "Mailboxes," he barreled on, "are all ugly, and most of them are pieces of junk. I want to make something different." He slid me a single sheet of paper with a drawing of an oblong, neon green and pink mailbox, complete with the unmistakable mailbox flag. "So, you want to make colorful mailboxes?" I asked. "Exactly," Dwight said, waving his fork, "and they're going to be durable and customizable and easy to buy. It's going to be great." That, however, is where the specifics ended. Despite spending thousands of dollars on engineering and concept renderings, Dwight couldn't give me more details on his business model. His concept wasn't exactly sketched on a napkin, but it wasn't far off.

While Dwight approached his problem from a different angle entirely — design first, plan later — he too lacked a clear value proposition. Terrance and Dwight aren't alone. Startups oversimplify or over-complicate their ideas all the time. On the surface, this may seem like a benign problem. After all, Mark Zuckerberg couldn't have known how Facebook would operate, much less how it would make money when he came up with the idea, right?

Let me distinguish between having a clear understanding of how an idea is supposed to create value for a consumer and knowing how all the pieces of a business model will fit together to make a profit. The latter is often an outgrowth of exploring the former — something startups unearth as they make products for customers and learn from those interactions. Zuckerberg, for example, had a clear understanding of the value he was creating even before he wrote the first line of code for Facebook. He was helping people connect online. Yes, that value evolved into Meta, the mega platform it is today. But, even at the beginning, Zuckerberg had the ever-important value proposition down; he knew who his customers were and what value he was creating for them.

Some founders can't whittle wild ideas down to their essential elements. Others can't describe multi-faceted ideas in concrete terms. This makes it hard to explain those ideas to other people. Nobody likes to be buried in information. Likewise, offering too little explanation leaves listeners wondering if what they're hearing is half-baked.

These mistakes lead to poor assumptions, wasted resources, and a whole lot of spinning. Being able to crisply explain an idea is key to making real progress.

This problem plagues entrepreneurs of all kinds, from sophisticated startups at Silicon Valley accelerators to corporate innovators at Fortune 500 companies. Whether in software or biotech, cosmetics, or clothing, it is difficult for innovators to succinctly explain the value of an early-stage idea.

Why is that? There are many reasons, but I've observed three repeatedly:

First, innovators frequently start by tackling their to-do lists. Developing product concepts, picking a name, recruiting a co-founder, launching a website, finding a lawyer, registering the company, building a prototype, filing for a patent, seeking mentors, lining up a supply chain, buying advertising, securing retail space, setting prices, responding to customers, landing investors — the tasks go on and on. Amid all that noise and hustling, innovators don't pause to clarify how they are creating value. Time and again I've asked busy founders simple questions about their strategies only to be met with "ums," "uhs," and uncomfortable silences.

Second, innovators struggle to simplify complex concepts because they have vastly more topical experience, context, and information than most people. This is the Curse of Knowledge — knowing so much about something that your explanation goes right over the audience's head.

Even if they know how to convey the basics, innovators sometimes use big words and technical jargon as armor against critics. Intimidating vocabulary can seem more credible, which might just keep people from asking nettlesome questions. But creating impediments that make it harder for others to understand an idea is the opposite of progress. When someone quickly "gets it," they'll be more likely to become a partner, advocate, or customer. But all too often, expert entrepreneurs end up bewildering rather than enlightening or engaging people.

Finally, innovators typically aren't eager to limit their ideas. "You have no vision," one entrepreneur once told me when I tried to simplify his startup's central mission. "We're going to revolutionize this industry! Everyone's going to want our product, and you're trying to put us into a box!" Asking entrepreneurs with ambitious dreams to explain the value they're creating in a few neat sentences, sometimes earns me a prickly response. This is partly because founders tend to be big thinkers and partly because committing to one path is scary. It's comforting to preserve multiple options. Unfortunately, avoiding focus is a big mistake for most founders. Startups are working with limited funds, and corporate innovators are working with limited goodwill. Both must use those resources wisely to break through the cacophony of voices competing for a consumer's attention.

Being unmistakably clear is crucial. As a buyer at Target, I saw first-hand how little time consumers spend considering a purchase. Even in my category, televisions, I was shocked at how quickly shoppers would make decisions. A few seconds determined whether they bought something or moved on. The average consumer's attention span passes from item to item in a flash. Entrepreneurs usually think their products warrant a few extra seconds, but that's just not the case.

It takes effort to understand new things and decide whether they're worth paying for. Who wants added stress in an already hurried, expensive shopping trip? Who wants to wade through pages of new products on an e-commerce site? That's just as true when a business needs to make a purchase. Whether companies are restocking office supplies, ordering raw materials, or integrating a new software system, it's natural to take expedient shortcuts, buy known quantities, and avoid unclear options. True, some purchases warrant a lot more research than others. But that makes it even more important to explain your value with vivid clarity. Anyone who has done their research will know value when they see it and likely have little tolerance for confusing concepts or solutions.

That's why having a sharp value message matters. Unknown brands need it to break through the noise and overcome the barriers of habit and inertia. Vague, broad, or confusing products rarely sell. Consumers are willing to dedicate shockingly scant time to new options. Squandering what precious little consideration comes your way is a bad idea.

All this leads to the kinds of mistakes innovators can least afford, wasted time and money. A confusing marketing message won't work. A fuzzy pitch will turn off investors. A vague strategy will de-motivate a team. That's all extremely costly.

But it doesn't have to be that way.

2.2 Build Your Foundation

A good value proposition promises to solve a specific customer's problem in a novel way. It implies a deep understanding of that customer and the competitive alternatives available to them.

It's also clear and concise. After all, if the consumer doesn't "get it" or doesn't have time to get it, they aren't buying it.

A well-built value proposition is powerful for two reasons: First, as the name implies, it describes how and why you believe your idea will create value. Second, it helps you identify the critical guesses you're making, which allows you to test them, which means fewer costly errors in time, energy, and financial investment. We'll discuss that further in the coming chapters.

To start, I break the value proposition into four "value hypothesis" questions, which, when answered, distill an idea down to its most essential elements:

- Who will be your first customer?
- What problem are you solving?
- What unique product are you offering?
- What special assets does your team have?

Visually, I arrange them into four connected boxes that form the foundation of the Value Proposition Matrix (VPM):

Customer | Team

| Who will be your first customer? | What special assets does your team have? |
| What problem are you solving? | What unique product are you offering? |

Problem | Solution

While there are countless questions to answer at the beginning of a new venture, these four form the core of value creation. Like the four walls of a foundation, every other aspect of innovation is built on top of these questions.

Why these four? Put in the simplest terms, customers pay companies (teams) to solve their problems. Pricing, channels, partners, suppliers, manufacturing, marketing — all of these are just support mechanisms a company uses to solve that problem for (hopefully, more and more) customers and make money in return. All can be, and almost always are, adjusted to meet demand.

Everything flows from this fundamental value equation.

Of course, getting this equation right doesn't guarantee a winning business. Pricing, channels, and all the rest still need to work in concert to deliver a profitable, durable business model. However, building a strategy based on a mistaken connection between the customer, their problem, your unique solution, and the team behind it is nearly always going to lead a venture to ruin.

It's worth taking a moment to note that quite a few innovators have gotten very rich without consciously answering these four value proposition questions. They had an idea and built it. It sold, and they became successful. Sometimes it is that simple. Seeking to answer these questions does not guarantee success. This method is, rather, a way of amplifying your chances of succeeding while limiting your risk. A sound strategy won't guarantee success for an entrepreneur or intrapreneur, but it will significantly improve the odds. That is what these questions provide — a framework to systematically map a path to value creation.

Let's explore the questions individually to unpack what makes them so powerful and discuss how to answer each.

2.3 Find Your Niche

The Customer

When I ask innovators who they think their customers will be, the answer I typically get is "Everyone." But when a first-time entrepreneur named Carla came to MAGNET with her idea, she was laser-focused on her target. "My product is for people who have a hard time dressing and undressing," she said. Carla makes a special type of clothing called adaptive apparel, which fastens and folds in ways that make it easier to put on and take off. More precisely, Carla's clothing is designed for elderly people with debilitating mental or physical conditions like Alzheimer's and dementia.

I was impressed with Carla's willingness to pick such a specific consumer segment. She was following **the most important rule when choosing a new target: focus on a niche.** Volumes have been written about the wisdom of starting with a niche, most famously in the groundbreaking work by Joe Bohlen, George Beal, and Everett Rogers on the Innovation Adoption Curve. Rogers argues that consumers adopt innovations in groups. These groups fit into a normal bell curve, starting with what he calls Innovators and Early Adopters, moving to broader adoption by the Early and Late Majority, and finally becoming widely accepted by consumers they call Laggards.

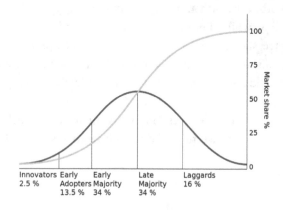

History has shown that finding and focusing on Roger's "innovators" and "early adopters" gives an entrepreneur the best chance of breaking into a market. This is called a niche strategy. I won't presume to add anything new to that well-worn discussion, but I'll summarize the concept for readers who aren't familiar with this approach or need a refresher.

Designing a product requires trade-offs. Do you choose the expensive material and raise your price, or select the cheaper material and keep the price down? Do you offer one color and streamline your production process or produce an array of colors and make your process more complicated? Do you add lots of features and, with them, lengthy instructions, or do you simplify the product and make it easier to use? Every product development decision comes at a cost. If you're designing for a broad category of consumers (think Millennials, Moms, or the dreaded "Everyone"), deciding which costs to incur and which to forgo is tricky. There are simply too many types of people and preferences within those large groups.

Trying to make everyone happy is notoriously ill-advised, especially as a startup with limited resources. Sure, a giant company like Apple can build a few types of iPhones that make hundreds of millions of people happy, but Apple has earned that ability over decades. In fact, all of Apple's success started by focusing on a niche. When Apple co-founders, Steve Jobs and Steve Wozniak, launched the Apple II in 1977, they hoped that a few hobbyists would be interested in buying a personal computer.

At the time, tech stalwarts like IBM were building computers for businesses, ignoring the tiny fraction of the population using computers at home. Apple's initial market was so small that the US Census Bureau wouldn't even start tracking household computer use until 1984. Even then, only 8.4% of US homes had computers. Nearly a decade after its founding, Apple was still developing products for a niche consumer. Some argue that they still are. The first iPod, iPhone, and Apple Watch (with pre-orders surpassing two million) targeted young adults and millennial parents — probably as large as a niche should get.

But it's because big companies like Apple can eventually target huge groups that it's better for startups to focus on narrow niches. Large companies usually avoid fixating on small groups of consumers. Burdened by established growth expectations, big companies overlook or lump together small segments because their leaders and shareholders demand bigger revenue opportunities and higher margins. Underserved groups may look small to big companies, but they can be very appealing to startups. This is precisely what drives disruption.

As Clayton Christensen puts it in his seminal work on disruption, *The Innovator's Dilemma*, "Disruptive technologies bring to a market a very different value proposition than had been available previously. Generally, disruptive technologies underperform established products in mainstream markets. But they have other features that a few fringe (and generally new) customers value." In other words, niche products don't appeal to everyone, but the people they do appeal to love them. Focusing on these underserved niches is where new ventures can thrive.

Large companies often overlook thin slivers of the market but, ironically, they can be rather easy to find. Consumers with niche needs and interests like to shop at particular retailers, get their information from specific sources, and spend their time doing unconventional things. Computer hobbyists weren't that hard for Jobs and Wozniak to find in the late 70s, just like tech-savvy enclaves or cutting-edge fashion mavens aren't hard to find today. They're outliers, and their interests, habits, and geographies make them stand out. That means if a startup knows where to look, it can capture a niche's attention without a corporate-sized advertising budget.

Perhaps most importantly, niches are more likely to buy a product that meets their specialized needs. Eager, largely ignored consumers love products that are designed just for them.

That affinity, in turn, makes it harder for competitors to dislodge a specialized brand, even when the niche grows. That leaves a natural market opportunity and is often the way new ventures find early traction.

A niche is, by definition, narrow. A lot of innovators worry that a narrow focus limits their revenue potential. That's true; it does. But that's good. By going after a niche, innovators are less likely to invite competition. That sets up an opportunity to establish a base of loyal initial consumers (early adopters). Expanding beyond a narrow base of superfans is how countless large companies (like Apple) got started. It's difficult to find examples of successful companies that didn't start with a narrow, highly engaged group of consumers in mind. Everyone must start somewhere, and the best place to start is with a niche.

If you're struggling to narrow your target, ask these three questions:

1. Who will love this product?
2. Who won't mind what's imperfect about it?
3. Who have the established competitors neglected?

Innovators are sometimes quick to make guesses here, assuming they understand their target. But often, they don't, at least not deeply and without biases. If you haven't had dozens of conversations with your target customers, you probably don't have enough information to know whether they'll love your product, what they're willing to overlook, and what alternatives are already addressing their needs.

Don't be afraid to sharpen your target. Remember, these are your early adopters, not the only people who will ever buy your product.

For example, Ezra invented an app that allows users to better organize and prioritize incoming communications. He hoped this would reduce the constant distractions that pull people away from their personal and professional relationships.

When my team at MAGNET began working with Ezra, he was certain that his niche was young moms who wanted to be more attentive to their families. As of 2021, there were nearly 35 million mothers with children under 18 in the US. To give you a reference point, Target Corp., a $70 billion retail giant, says that they focus on moms. That's an enormous market, far too large for a small startup. Instead, we worked with Ezra to find a smaller niche by asking the three targeting questions: who might love what was great about his product, not mind its shortcomings, and was small enough to be overlooked by larger competitors?

We decided his technology might be best suited for people who have a great deal of demand on their time, are invested in fostering relationships, and are willing to serve as an example to others. To us, religious leaders fit this profile exactly. Ezra, a Rabbi himself, was connected to a network of 4,000 such leaders, some of whom had already expressed interest in his technology. Thus, we adjusted his initial target down from 35 million mothers to 4,000 religious leaders. When compared with moms, Ezra's new target was far more likely to love what was great about his product and look past its limitations. Better yet, very few tech products focus on religious leaders. Ultimately, this was the target he chose, and where he found his earliest and most enthusiastic adopters.

Defining and narrowing your early adopters is crucial to any upstart innovation effort. While your target may evolve as you learn more about your market, it's critical to train your energy on building products for your core consumer; which makes it imperative to understand the problem you're solving for them.

2.4 Not All Problems Are Created Equal

The Problem
What separates a good idea from a bad idea? I meet smart innovators working on creative ideas every day. But frequently, what holds them back is not the quality of the product or ser-

vice they're developing; rather, it's the quality of the problem they're trying to solve. That's why **one of the most important aspects of any value proposition is a meaningful problem.**

How do I define a "problem"? A problem is friction, inefficiency, frustration, irritation, or delay. It's a cost that an individual or organization endures. Problems are ubiquitous, encountered by all of us every day. Problems range from the universal and profoundly painful — disease, poverty, addiction, natural disaster — to the specific and relatively minor; a noisy neighbor, a slow website, a flat tire, or a dull razor blade. Some problems are felt mostly by consumers, while others are felt largely by businesses. Problems are also infinite. A solution creates other problems. The first car fixed the problems with using horses as vehicles (they die, poop, etc.), but it created problems of its own (traffic, auto accidents, pollution, and many more).

If an endless supply of problems excites you, congratulations, you're an innovator. But not all problems are created equal, and finding the good ones is no small feat.

What separates a good problem from a not-so-good one? This is debatable. However, I recommend solving problems that, with some generous latitude, are *solvable, scalable, and significant.*

Solvable problems

Obviously, any problem worth solving must be solvable. If you're an optimist, you may find yourself scoffing at this statement. After all, humanity solved many problems that seemed intractable before they were solved. But, by solvable, I don't mean possible. I mean, simply, that if you're an innovator, you must be able to describe the problem with enough granularity to act. "World hunger" is a problem. But getting that down to a solvable level requires far more segmentation.

To whittle a big problem down to a small one, I recommend asking a version of the Five Whys, a technique developed at Toyota to find the root of a problem. When you're looking for a solvable problem, and you're starting with something like world hunger, ask "How might we ..." five times:

1. How might we solve world hunger? Perhaps by increasing crop production.
2. How might we increase crop production? Perhaps by irrigating more land.
3. How might we irrigate more land? Perhaps by watering more efficiently.
4. How might we water more efficiently? Perhaps by monitoring water content in soil.
5. How might we monitor water content in soil? Perhaps by developing better agricultural sensors.

While the "how might we/perhaps by" exercise can continue, typically, five rounds will help a team distill their problem into a more solvable idea. As you can see, developing better agricultural sensors is imminently more solvable (albeit still difficult) than eliminating world hunger. This is, of course, one idea among many. The Five Whys should help generate many possibilities.

Dream big. But leave grand problem statements to politicians and philosophers. Innovators get things done, and to do that, they need tangible problems to solve.

Scalable problems
Asking whether a problem is scalable is the mirror image of the solvable question. In other words, while a problem shouldn't be impossibly big, it should also be substantial enough, either now or in the future, to earn meaningful consumer engagement.

I frequently see innovators solving problems that few people have and which are unlikely to become important problems in the future. Someone, after all, must be willing to pay to solve this problem. The bigger the problem, the more it's worth. The price someone is willing to pay multiplied by the number of people willing to pay equals revenue. If that number is too small or will take too long to build and attract investors, the idea is probably a hobby or a passion project, not a scalable business.

This may sound simple, but I've seen hundreds of ideas that miss the mark. One student approached me with an idea to develop software that helped organic farmers more efficiently track and file US regulatory paperwork. The USDA counted over 16,500 certified organic farms in the US in 2019 at a whopping 14.5% annual growth rate. That seems like a market worth exploring. However, this entrepreneur believed farmers would need to use this software once every three years and that it would be worth about $200 per use. Even with a healthy 25% market share and a double-digit growth rate, projections for this business fell well below $300k in annual revenue. For a software business that would need to attract investors and keep continuous track of complex regulations, this problem did not pass the scalability test.

Be careful not to confuse this with your early adopter niche. Yes, focus on a few highly engaged consumers early on. But also keep your eye on the market potential. Jobs and Wozniack started by focusing on techy personal computer hobbyists but believed everyone could feasibly want a computer in their home one day. If the potential size of a market remains small, the problem you're solving might not be big enough.

The example of organic farmers and their paperwork problems might look different if this was a problem *all* farmers faced, or one they might face in the coming years. Technology, consumer tastes, regulations, and global trade dynamics all play a part in determining the trajectory of a problem's scale.

A thin line separates the right niche and a niche that's too small; to understand the difference, it's important to recall the adoption curve discussed earlier. For a niche to be powerful, there needs to be a high and wide wave of consumers poised to adopt a new product once it's established. If the adoption curve looks less like a mountain and more like a long, low hill, it means that there simply aren't enough people who make up the total market for the early niche to morph into a sizable customer base.

For example, the tiny number of consumers who opted to buy the first electric vehicles were a harbinger of a massive potential market because billions of people own cars. By comparison, software that translates Old English into Latin might attract some enthusiastic early adopters. Still, the pool of consumers who might eventually follow those first adopters simply isn't large enough — without expanding the product's capabilities — to sustain growth.

Significant problems

Just as a problem should be solvable and scalable, it should also be important enough to motivate action. In other words, find problems that are significant. Generally, significant problems call to mind words or phrases like expensive, time-consuming, frustrating, or ineffective. These describe pains and frictions with the current solutions. If a problem isn't significant enough, converting target customers to a new product or service will be a challenge. Why change course when things are good enough? The cost of swapping the known for the unknown may be too great, or customers will simply be too unmotivated to try the alternative.

It's fair to think, "Wait, isn't a better product worth exploring?" Often, yes. But innovators are prone to believe that every product improvement provides enough opportunity to build a successful business. But simply solving any problem in a better way isn't a ticket to entrepreneurial paradise; solving the *right* problem, however, is a very good start. In a world where retailers, content peddlers, advertisers, and social media sites are competing for every moment of our attention, solving a significant problem gives innovators a better chance to stand out or, better yet, be found.

But is every product really solving a problem? When I'm

encouraging innovators to solve significant problems, clients, classes, or audiences often produce examples of successful products that, they believe, don't solve problems at all. Candy Crush, Ferraris, the Pet Rock — what problems could these possibly be solving?

Video games solve one of the most important and lucrative problems to plague mankind — boredom. Video game players rave about a game's addictiveness or its "replayability." In other words, playing it doesn't get boring. Don't believe boredom is a problem? Consider your mental state the next time you open a social media app — there's a good chance you were bored and seeking a distraction when you reached for your phone. Likewise, luxury sports cars offer their drivers the chance to solve a problem that most of us would be lucky to have — how to get noticed. The Pet Rock? We all need something to laugh at and talk about. Every successful product solves a problem. However, problems aren't all equal in their significance.

Of course, it's not always easy to explain the problem you're solving. That's because problems come in layers. It's important to pull back several layers as you try to isolate the core of your problem. For example, one startup I met with explained they were creating an app to help people with complicated food requirements figure out which dishes would meet their needs when dining out.

The problem these founders were solving, they explained, was that it's hard to know which restaurants serve the kinds of foods that are friendly to certain diets and dietary restrictions. I asked for an example of how a customer might use their product. One founder explained, "If you're following a special diet, it can be embarrassing to ask the server about particular ingredients. Often, they don't know the answer, or they're wrong." Put this way, the root problem — the point at which the customer is feeling the pain — might not stem from the lack of information about a restaurant's food. Instead, the pain might be the awkwardness of an interaction with a server or appearing "picky" in front of friends and colleagues. Consumers, like these innovators, might assume that the best solution involves doing research ahead of time. But seeing the problem in a different light opens other possible solutions. For example, what if an app could use a mobile phone camera to scan a menu and make recommendations based on keywords? While this is certainly not the only possible solution (and it might not even be a very good one), it's built around a less obvious but perhaps more significant problem.

Digging into any problem to look for its root isolates what matters most to the consumer and, critically, informs the solution with exquisite focus.

2.5 The Fix

The Solution
Innovators love talking about their solutions. A fresh solution, after all, is a better, faster, stronger, or cheaper way to accomplish something. That's where innovators spend a great deal of their time and energy. Laboratories, R&D facilities, test kitchens, maker spaces, art studios, and garage workshops are built for that purpose. So, when I ask about a founder's solution, it's not surprising when I get long and enthusiastic explanations. Innovators gush about features, capabilities, design iterations, ingredients, specifications, performance metrics, tolerances, technological advancements, and origin stories.

When I gently ask for a distilled solution — ideally a sentence or two — I am usually met with uneasy stutters and meandering explanations. The same thought flashes across every furrowed brow, "But there's so much to say!"

To add a wrinkle, I sneak an extra word into my question. "Tell me about your *unique* solution in a sentence or two." Sometimes this helps. Focusing an innovator on what makes their solution special frees them from listing everything that makes it great. The discussion becomes more about explaining how it stands up to its alternatives. This is usually an easier task for innovators, though still challenging, as it intentionally leaves a lot of details behind.

That's ok. Solutions should be simple to explain. Anyone casually familiar with the category or industry ought to be able to quickly compare the concept to what exists. As we discussed in Chapter One, consumers have little patience for complicated or long-winded sales pitches. They want their problem solved, not an opus about why the solution is so great. If this is a challenge, I'll ask for a point of parity (how is the solution like the nearest alternative) and a point of difference (what makes it better)?

In 1973, low calorie beers were just making their market debut. Miller Lite's marketing team set out to explain how their new product competed with other beers and hit on one of the classic point-of-parity, point-of-difference claims: "Great taste, less filling." In other words, it tastes great, you know, like beer. But it's not full of so many heavy calories. Voila! A crystal-clear comparison. *AdAge* Magazine ranks Miller Lite's catchy comparison as the eighth-best advertising campaign in history. Explaining how something new stacks up against what exists along these two dimensions gets right to the heart of an idea.

Of course, an impactful comparison is only as good as the frame of reference, in this case, the competition. So, it's important to be intimately familiar with the alternative products or services. This can be more difficult than it seems.

In the most extreme cases, innovators believe their ideas have no competition. "This is the first one of its kind; there's nothing on the market like it," a team of entrepreneurs once told me. They were developing a new ranking system for foreign business schools. "Nobody has done this before, so we aren't competing against anyone." Unfortunately, this indicates two concerning possibilities.

First, if there is truly no competition at all, it can foreshadow too little demand. It's rare to find a market completely devoid of products or services. If a marketplace seems completely bereft of your concept, question why. Is it because this idea is truly the first of its kind, or is it the entrepreneurial equivalent of a ghost town — once settled but abandoned for one ominous reason or another? Hint: ideas are rarely completely new to the world.

The second and more likely possibility when an innovator sees no competition is that they simply haven't looked hard enough or considered all the ways a problem could be solved. For example, I worked with one inventor who was developing heavy-duty exercise equipment that could be easily adjusted to accommodate multiple users at the same time. He was convinced that there was nothing even remotely like this product on the market and, thus, he had no competition. However, he began to rethink that assertion when I asked whether buying more bench presses could accomplish the same outcome. His solution did have unique features beyond what additional equipment could offer, but it was wildly inaccurate to say he had no competition.

Innovators are also prone to insufficiently explore alternative solutions. This is a phenomenon I've seen over and over. Whether consciously or not, innovators often just don't do enough research on their competition. I've seen more than one inventor get a jolt when someone finds a comparable product they've somehow missed. Why is that?

As mentioned, an innovator can occasionally be so sure their idea is novel, they don't bother looking for competing ideas. For example, I was working with one innovator who wanted to develop a better way to care for bedridden patients. When I asked if she'd searched for competing patents, she said no but that she was confident nothing like her product existed. After all, she worked in a large hospital, and "they have everything," she said. "If they don't have something like this, it obviously doesn't exist." A Google search produced several similar concepts, as did a review of the US Patent Office's online database.

I've also seen plenty of examples where an innovator performs a cursory Google search, discovers nothing of note, and declares their concept unique. Unfortunately, not everyone uses the same search terms, and competing products don't always show up among the top results. Google is a powerful tool, but its algorithm has misled many innovators to believe their ideas are unrivaled.

Daniel Kahneman, a Nobel Prize-winning behavioral economist, and bias expert termed this the "what-you-see-is-all-there-is" phenomenon. Kahneman argued that human beings naturally believe that their immediate surroundings represent the world as a whole. This simple mental model helps us make sense of our complex surroundings. "You will often find," Kahneman explains, "that knowing little makes it easier to fit everything you know into a coherent pattern." He goes on to explain that human beings are predisposed to jump to all sorts of conclusions based on what they see right in front of them. Worse, they unconsciously seek more evidence to support what they believe is true and avoid evidence that contradicts their beliefs. We'll further explore Kahneman's work on biases (and how they can hamstring innovators) in Chapter Seven.

Of course, a unique solution is not the only thing that allows innovators to distinguish their ideas from the rest. Innovators themselves can bring an essential dimension to the value proposition.

2.6 All Together Now!

The Team

As challenging as questions about the customer, problem, and solution can be, they rarely surprise innovators. All three tend to show up in some form in early conversations. However, when I ask, "Why are you uniquely positioned to bring this idea to life?" I tend to get a wide range of reactions. Everything from indignation, "Because it's my idea!" to anger, "Are you saying I can't do this?!", to confusion, "I don't understand why that matters.", and dejection, "Not much, I guess.", from caution, "I think I have some real assets.", to confidence "I have what matters most — I'm committed!"

I'll then ask the innovator to list the assets — their own or their team's — that can help them achieve their vision. This might include:

- Skills and expertise
- Prior experience
- Existing customer relationships
- Networks and connections
- Investments and financing
- Concepts and prototypes
- Mentors and support structures
- Intellectual property or trade secrets
- Certifications or licenses
- Brand awareness
- An established website
- An audience/followers
- Unique sources of supply
- Manufacturing capability
- Inventory

You might notice that the idea itself is not listed above. An idea alone has no real value. This can startle innovators, who often treasure and carefully guard their ideas. I've been asked to sign non-disclosure agreements more times than I can count, sometimes by innovators without so much as a drawing of their concept. **But an idea is only valuable if someone can bring it to life. That requires the right combination of assets and skills.**

I broadly categorize this topic as "Team" because, whether in the form of a dedicated group or that of a solo entrepreneur with a support network (mentors, investors, subcontractors), every company or product is brought to life by a team.

But if that's true, why do so many innovators rarely stop to ask, "Why me?" or, "Why us?"

In part, I believe it's because technology makes it easier than ever to connect with people and find resources. Fifty years ago, it might've been nearly impossible to collaborate with a global team, but today, modern communication puts a whole world of talent at our fingertips.

But despite the far-reaches of LinkedIn and Google, in practice, it's still difficult to find the *right* people to bring an idea to life. Anyone who ever thought it would be a snap to find someone to write Python code, program a Raspberry Pi, navigate food safety regulations, file a utility patent, design a great digital marketing campaign, or contribute early-stage seed funding knows otherwise. It's hard work assembling the right team and forging relationships that can stand the strain of creating something new.

While it's tough to find a great team, it's just as hard to acquire protectable assets. Patents — if an idea is patentable at all — take years to get and often cost thousands of dollars. Prototypes and capital equipment, particularly if it's custom-built or modified, are expensive too. Digital assets, like functional code, engaged followers, and quality email addresses, are hard-earned. Assuming it will be easy to gather the necessary assets is rather naive.

Corporate innovators fall into this trap as easily as startups. Charged with accomplishing a herculean task — building something new within an existing organization — it can seem as though the one thing working in an intrapreneur's favor is access to lots of resources. Yet, in many cases, those resources are spoken for or withheld from projects that look risky. Why take money and people away from the core business to fund the unknown? Thus, money and talent can quickly become just as scarce for innovators inside large companies as they can for startups.

Ideas aren't keys, so much as seeds. Seeds contain incredible possibilities, but they only grow if they're planted in the right soil and given the right nutrients. So too, ideas only grow into thriving businesses if they're cultivated by the right team.

When Rahul, a young entrepreneur, began talking to me about starting an apparel business, he didn't have an essential skill for someone in fashion design; the ability to cut cloth into patterns and sew it into clothing. Even so, he had some other important assets — an eye for style, a background in apparel retail, and lots of hands-on experience helping startups. "I felt like as long as I was actively working to shore up the missing pieces of my skill set, I was still working in a space where I could succeed," Rahul said. With a borrowed sewing machine, he began teaching himself the basics of making clothing. He also started networking with successful apparel entrepreneurs and designers, learning from their journeys. He knew where he was strong and which assets he needed to build to set his business up for success.

Of course, it's possible to start a business without knowing a lot about the product or service you plan to create. But, if that's the case, something else about the business should be uniquely suited to you and your team. Are you deeply passionate about solving a particular problem? Have you inherited a business that could grow in a new direction? Does your prior experience help illuminate a market opportunity that others might not see? If, instead, you simply believe you can build a better mousetrap because inspiration struck you, consider the difficult path on which you're about to embark.

"Know thyself" was inscribed on the Temple of Apollo at Delphi, the home of the famed oracle. This guidance is just as apt for modern innovators as it was for ancient Greeks. To succeed, an innovator must know what advantages they have and what help they need. Nobody does it alone, but entrepreneurs make a mistake if they assume their skills and assets aren't important factors in their success. Likewise, they make a mistake in assuming the skills and assets they don't have are easy to obtain.

There is an oft-repeated story in startup circles about "the entrepreneur who started with nothing." The story goes that an entrepreneur began with a few dollars and a dream. With hard work and determination, that dream became a reality. The moral of the story is that with an idea, grit, and effort, an innovator can accomplish anything. It's an appealing story that is rooted deep within a capitalist belief system that venerates self-reliance and innovation. It's a powerful and inspiring narrative that has driven countless entrepreneurs to great heights. Unfortunately, it's almost always an incomplete picture of how innovations take flight.

Success takes more than an idea and will. Whether with capital, connections, expertise, or intellectual property, or some other hard-won advantage, successful innovators almost universally have a unique constellation of assets. Conversely, I can list dozens upon dozens of entrepreneurs who I've seen labor under the false assumption that they can force any innovation into the world.

By no means is this a cautionary tale meant to dissuade passionate entrepreneurs. Passion is the bedrock of every innovative pursuit. However, I hope to help right-size notions about the extent to which "a dream and hard work" are all anyone needs to build a business. They are necessary but not sufficient in and of themselves. Solid innovation efforts are built with such qualities. But they are built on each innovator's unique assets and advantages. Understanding and harnessing what sets them apart will make all the difference in an innovator's quest to turn an idea into a thriving business.

2.7 Putting the Pieces Together

Let's take another look at the VPM, now that we've explored each of its four components in detail:

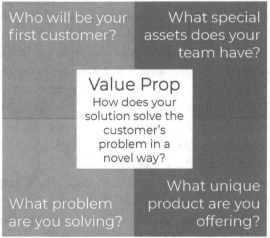

Who will be your first customer?

What problem are you solving?

What unique product are you offering?

What special assets does your team have?

The sum of these four questions explains how you and your team plan to solve a specific customer's problem uniquely — in a way that sets your solution apart from the competition. In other words, this is your value proposition.

To put things into context, we'll use the matrix to summarize the value proposition of a fabulously successful startup, Dollar Shave Club.

In 2011 Michael Dubin and Mark Levine founded a scrappy new company that aimed to fix a baffling problem — the high price of razors. Over the past several decades, razor blade giant Gillette expanded its market share by offering higher-priced razors with increasingly complex features like multiple blades, lubrication strips, hinging heads, premium grips, and vibration. The strategy was simple; introduce a new feature and increase the price of the product, selling replacement blades for an extravagant premium (the suggested retail price for a single blade was often more than $5). Enticed by fat margins, retailers offered Gillette more and more shelf space, limiting competition. What's more, many of these blades were so expensive that some retailers opted to lock them in cases. This made shopping for razor blades a particularly painful experience.

Dubin and Levine sought to circumvent these problems by selling razor blades online. Today that might seem obvious, but at the time, consumers were just getting acquainted with e-commerce. What's more, the two entrepreneurs decided to offer their products in a subscription format. For a low monthly price ($1 plus shipping), Dollar Shave Club would ship its customers a starter kit, including a razor handle and four replacement blades. Four more replacement blades would show up the following month. The fledgling company's YouTube video asked, "Do you like spending $20 a month on name-brand razors? Does your razor need a vibrating handle, a flashlight, a back scratcher, and ten blades?" Millions of people viewed that video and loved what they saw. The rest is history.

In 2016 Unilever acquired Dollar Shave Club for more than $1 billion. The following year *The Wall Street Journal* reported that Gillette was slashing the average price of its razors by up to 20%.

Dollar Shave Club's marketing material, including its You-Tube video, presents each of the four value proposition questions like this:

Customer: Young men who shave frequently

Problem: Retail razor blades are too expensive

Solution: Inexpensive razor blades delivered every month

Team: Low overhead, marketing expertise, inventory, established logistics

Combined, the value proposition can be stated this way:

Dollar Shave Club (DSC) saves young men money by shipping great blades without all the expensive overhead.

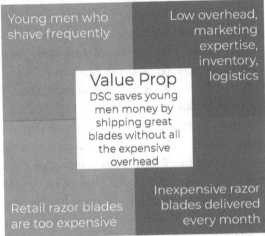

This simple value proposition was the cornerstone of Dollar Shave Club's highly successful business model. The components each fit neatly together like puzzle pieces, supporting a coherent, powerful consumer promise. What's more, the Dollar Shave Club founders clearly went through a value-defining exercise in line with the core value questions set out at the beginning of this chapter. The customer is well-defined, (note: it's not "all people who shave") the problem is significant, the solution is simple but unique, and the team had the right mix of assets to bring the idea to life.

Innovators commonly ask which question I recommend as a starting point, but every innovation journey is different, so prescribing one universal starting point isn't realistic.

Classically, innovators begin by identifying a problem, then focusing on a niche group that feels that problem most acutely.

(You'll often hear innovators say something like, "fall in love with the problem, not the solution.") From there, they'll seek solutions that fit their team's skill set. Some innovators may start with their core set of skills and assets, then branch out to customers, problems, and unique solutions that fit those unique capabilities. It's also possible to start with a solution and seek a problem to solve. 3M did this with great success when they discovered that an adhesive they'd developed was perfect for applying and reapplying paper to other objects (a product that eventually became the Post-it Note.) Finally, it's possible to start with a niche group of consumers and seek to solve their problems. Innovators sometimes observe consumers in action and address the issues they encounter.

Wherever you start, however, you should know that your initial hypothesis about how the four components of value fit together, is almost guaranteed to be wrong. Or at the very least, can be greatly improved. We'll spend the rest of the book discussing how to better understand the crucial guesses innovators make and how to root out potential blind spots.

Chapter Three
What You Know for Sure that Just Ain't So

Synopsis: The Value Proposition Matrix can help quickly identify the four assumptions at the heart of any new business model. These are:

1. That it is addressing a **burning problem**
2. That it **uniquely solves** the customer's problem
3. That the team can **deliver** this unique solution
4. That the team can **convert** the customer

This is more than a list of guesses; it's a map guiding innovators to where they should spend their limited time, energy, and resources.

3.1 Fundamental Assumptions

"It ain't what you don't know that gets you into trouble.
It's what you know for sure that just ain't so."
— Mark Twain (maybe)

"As we know, there are known knowns; there are things we know that
we know. We also know there are known unknowns; that is to say,

*we know there are some things we do not know. But there are also
unknown unknowns. The ones we don't know we don't know.
... It's the latter category that tends to be the difficult ones."*

— Donald Rumsfeld, Former US Secretary of Defense

Jane is an energy scientist. After years of working for a large technology company, she designed a small energy storage device that she believed to be far better than the industry-leading battery. It's clean, compact, and best of all, highly efficient. For every hour's worth of energy the competing product can deliver, Jane's technology would be able to deliver ten times that amount.

There are just a few problems. Jane doesn't have a working prototype, and assembling one will take hundreds of thousands of dollars. Unfortunately, she doesn't have investors yet, nor does she know any. Companies might be interested in licensing her idea, but she worries they might be just as likely to try and steal it from her. On the other hand, she doesn't know exactly how to commercialize this technology or how profitable it could potentially be. Not having anything to sell, of course, she doesn't have any customers. While she is confident many people would pay for a product like hers, she's not sure where to find her first buyer. Does she try selling directly to consumers? Could she be a supplier to a larger manufacturer? Would the military want it? She has this amazing idea, but what in the world should she do next?

Jane's story is all too familiar. Innovators often find themselves asking many of the same questions. Mostly, they boil down to "What should I do next?" With so many unknowns, they're often in need of a plan and a clear path forward.

Unknowns can be paralyzing because every unknown requires at least one corresponding guess. Not sure what price customers might be willing to pay for your product? Before you know, you guess. There are countless unknowns just like that in early-stage innovation.

To use Donald Rumsfeld's infamously cumbersome phrase,

there are also unknown unknowns — the hidden or uncontemplated assumptions that cause problems when they reveal themselves down the line.

Whether a founder pitching for a multi-million-dollar Series A investment or a team of corporate innovators sketching early ideas on whiteboard, guesses — both known and unknown — are the bedrock of any new venture and the source of your success (or potential failure).

Just four critical assumptions sit at the center of every business model. These four assumptions correspond to the four value proposition questions introduced in the last chapter. If the Value Proposition Matrix describes the heart of value creation, the assumptions that link those components together are, in turn, fundamental to the innovation process.

Knowing and testing these assumptions provides powerful insights, unmasking unknown unknowns. It also cuts the swarm of guesses down to a manageable handful.

This is the key to helping Jane, our friend the energy scientist. There are things she knows, things she doesn't, and a lot of ground to cover in between to turn her idea into a business. Without a plan, she could easily find herself working on whatever is in front of her indefinitely; answering the next email, writing the next line of code, making the next calculation. All the while, bigger questions about the customer, the problem, the solution, and the team remain unanswered.

Instead, she could attempt to answer the four key questions, identify the most important guesses she's making, and begin working on those assumptions. If she finds that she's made an incorrect assumption, she'll know there's a flaw at the heart of her business model. She'll be able to adjust her value proposition and try again or pivot completely. Rather than flailing from one random to-do to the next, she'll have a clear plan. If she gets lost, she can always re-center herself on her value proposition.

So, if it's all about working on the right assumptions, where do we go to find them?

We can use the Value Proposition Matrix. Each VPM question touches its neighbor, creating four intersections between each quadrant: Customer and Problem, Problem and Solution, Solution and Team, and Team and Customer. Each intersection represents a key assumption.

Consider the target customer and the problem they want to solve. On the VPM, you'll find the intersection between the questions "Who will be your first customer?" and "What problem are you solving?" (See Figure 1):

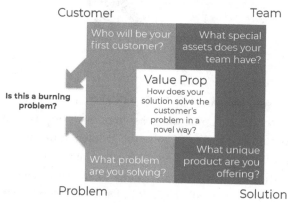

Figure 1

An assumption sits at the intersection of these two questions: that your target customer has that problem. We can dive deeper by asking if it is an important or "burning" problem. In Jane's example, she can talk to customers to uncover whether the inefficiency of their current batteries is enough of a problem to seek an alternative. Perhaps she'll learn that the size of batteries is more frustrating to potential customers and can opt to develop smaller products.

A second assumption relates to both the problem and the solution, and can be found between the questions "What problem are you solving?" and "What unique product are you offering?" (See Figure 2).

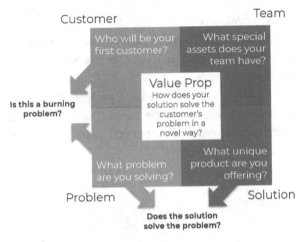

Figure 2

Does the solution solve the problem? This may sound obvious (that's the tricky thing about assumptions), but to be a solution, your product needs to solve the problem it intends to solve. That is to say, it needs to work. Ideally, the way it works is unique, setting it apart from the competition. Jane believes her device will work, and she has a lot of scientific knowledge to back that up. But until she builds a working prototype, she's still just making an educated guess. Even if her science is sound, solving a customer's problem is more than chemical reactions and material composition. It's about ensuring that the way the product works is good enough to get the job done in a manner that makes a consumer prefer to use it over the alternatives. Solving a problem on paper is very different from solving it in practice.

The third assumption sits between the unique solution and the team, at the intersection of the questions "What unique product are you offering?" and "What special assets does your team have?" (See Figure 3). The team must be able to create and deliver the solution using its special constellation of assets.

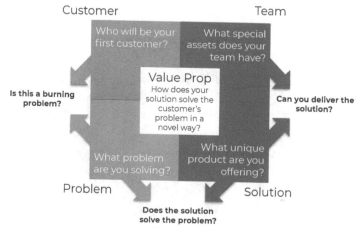

Figure 3

Jane might have a lot of knowledge about energy storage, but does she have a team that can help her turn her idea into a successful business? Money, connections, intellectual property, manufacturing know-how, even a basic financial model — these are all things that Jane will need if she's going to make and deliver her product to the market.

Finally, the fourth assumption addresses the two questions "What special assets does your team have?" and "Who will be your first customer?" (See Figure 4). The assumption made here is that the team must be able to convert the customer. In other words, the available assets and capabilities must put the team in a position to sell the product to the target, and the target must want to buy the product.

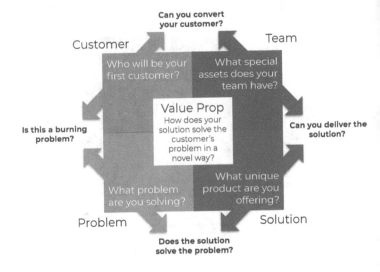

Figure 4

I mentioned that Jane believes "lots of people would pay for her product." But she doesn't know this for sure. Since she hasn't defined who exactly these nameless "people" are, how certain can she be that they (or anyone) will pay for her product? Confidence is not validation — especially what it comes to consumer behavior.

Collectively, these four assumptions represent the guesses upon which every value proposition is built, and all four have far-reaching implications for any new business.

In Jane's case, using the VPM helped her isolate these four simple yet crucial questions:

- Is her energy device solving an important problem for a clear early adopter?
- Does it work?
- Has she built the team and gathered the resources to deliver her technology?
- Will someone pay for it?

Prioritizing these four questions both narrows the scope of her work and crystallizes the answers she needs to find.

In this chapter, we'll unpack each assumption to better understand its implications. (In Chapter Four, we'll discuss some of the ways innovators can vet these assumptions.)

3.2 Is This a Burning Problem?

Sarah and Dan make and sell an industrial hand cleaner. For decades a small, loyal customer base of mechanics, road crews, and other blue-collar professionals have used their product. It's great at getting stubborn grime, paste, caulk, goo, oil, and myriad types of gunk off hands and tools. But recently, competition and an aging group of core users have started to erode sales. With this in mind, Sarah and Dan asked my team at MAGNET to help them explore whether their versatile product could be repurposed for a new market.

We set off on an atypical mission: to find a problem we could solve with an existing solution. We started by listing as many places as we could think of where tough gunk and grime get on hands and tools. After sorting that long list by what seemed to be the most promising customer base, Sarah and Danwent out and started learning about potential new customers' problems. As they did, they replicated one gooey, grimy situation after another to see if their cleaner might offer a better fix than the existing alternatives.

After several iterations, a friend told Sarah and Dan that their product might prove useful in an area neither knew anything about — small-scale marijuana harvesting. The friend went on to explain that cutting and handling marijuana plants was a messy process. The sticky, smelly resin from the plant's buds coated hands, scissors, jars — anything it touched. The resin would then harden into a spotty film, leaving harvesters with interminably sticky hands and tools so gunky that they often had to be thrown away. The only chemical on the market that seemed to help was isopropyl alcohol and, even then, it would take hours of soaking and scrubbing for the chemical to work its way through the marijuana resin. Their product, Sarah and Dan learned, seemed almost magical in comparison. With a quick application and a few easy wipes, it took the pesky residue right off. Their friend was ecstatic; this product was perfect for the marijuana resin problem.

As discussed in Chapter Two, problems come in all shapes and sizes, and people feel problems with varying degrees of intensity. Some problems are mere annoyances, while others can be life-altering. The bigger and more painful the problem, the further the person experiencing it will go (or pay) for a solution. And so, finding nasty, gnawing, burning problems is a great way to create value.

With the occasional exception of artists and musicians, most innovators intuitively know that they're solving problems. They often think their concepts, services, or inventions will make the world a better place. Brimming with confidence, **they persistently overestimate the importance of the problem they're solving. If I had to choose one assumption that trips up innovators the most, this is it.**

Because innovators often have first-hand experience with the problem they're trying to solve, it's tempting — and exceedingly common — for them to assume others wrestle with the same problem. While this might be true, it might also be true that others do not feel the problem with the same intensity. This leads innovators to overestimate demand for their solution.

The flash of inspiration that strikes an innovator when they see the solution to a problem can also blind them to the true magnitude of the problem they're solving. The problem takes on outsized importance in their minds because the solution they envision is so exciting.

As noted earlier, the lack of market need is one of the most common reasons startups fail — and market need is directly related to the quality of the problem being solved. Innovators usually think they're solving an important problem when, all too often, they aren't, at least not in the eyes of their target consumer.

Why is this such a common mistake? Because innovators — like all human beings — fall victim to common cognitive biases. For example, innovators tend to place more importance on the feedback they receive early-on in their innovation process. They also rely too heavily on early intuitions and previous experiences and they tend to seek information that confirms their ideas or hypotheses. (We cover cognitive biases extensively Chapter 7.)

An innovator's ability to find important problems is also limited to what they've experienced. This might seem obvious, but the problems innovators see and feel first-hand naturally define the scope of the problems they set out to solve. This is why my students often set out to solve problems within or related to the student experience. Recurring concepts include services that help college students buy and sell furniture and software that helps students find jobs. Year after year, my students, just like innovators everywhere, tackle their own problems.

To be clear, addressing familiar problems isn't foolish. It can be a very good thing because, ostensibly, intimate knowledge of an issue might set an innovator's solution apart. However, when you find yourself saying, "I have this problem; others must too," you're making a seductive — but risky — assumption.

When Sarah and Dan told my team about their friend's compelling insights, we recommended that we figure out whether this was a problem that growers frequently experience or just their enthusiastic friend. In other words, we counseled them to vet whether they were addressing their target's burning problem.

It might've been tempting for Sarah and Dan to dive head-long into making the product, branding it, and marketing it. But after trying that approach with an idea that subsequently floundered, they knew to view their assumptions with suspicion. Because they were new to the marijuana industry and had received their key insight from a single consumer, they needed to start by understanding the relationship between small-scale marijuana growers and this sticky-hand-and-tools phenomenon. With that clear starting point in mind, it wasn't hard to focus their efforts. They talked to small-scale marijuana growers, experts in marijuana cultivation, and industrial-scale growers in states where cultivation was legal at the time. They found that, indeed, resin produced during the harvesting and processing of marijuana is a constant source of irritation. Exploring the problem and building on what they learned gave them the confidence to ramp up production, but it also sharpened their understanding of the industry. This helped them focus their marketing and product development efforts on small-scale growers, who seemed to find resin particularly vexing.

3.3 Does Your Unique Solution Solve the Problem?

Some of the critical assumptions we discuss in this chapter aren't always obvious to innovators. But convincing them to test whether their idea works is rarely an issue. From software and services to manufactured products and medical devices, innovators almost universally understand that their idea must deliver what it promises in a way that stands out.

Let's say you are developing an investment app. The most natural first step is to create a simple version of the software, then modify it until a consumer can buy, sell, and view different investments. That is reflexively a test of both whether the concept works and whether it's novel. Or, if you were developing an on-demand home maintenance business, you might test whether the concept works via a simple website through which a maintenance issue is reported and, in turn, the system can dispatch an expert to fix the problem.

Bringing an idea to life by building it is absolutely necessary. However, innovators often think this should be the extent of their efforts — to build the thing they envision and get it to work. But that's only one piece of the innovation puzzle. Judging whether something "works" is not up to the innovator — it's up to the customer. That means building an idea isn't simply about synthesizing it in a lab, writing the code, or building it with a 3D printer. Instead, it's about observing consumers as they use it to solve a problem. In that way, vetting whether a product works is an effort that should include your team, experts, AND customers. There's much more to come on the vetting process in the next chapter.

3.4 Can your team deliver?

When Bill Adler took over as CEO of True Fit, an e-commerce apparel startup, he saw the opportunity to transform the company's business model. To Bill, the company's unique way of collecting consumer data and turning it into fashion recommendations could become something much bigger. Rather than providing their narrow set of consumers with insightful clothing suggestions (in this case, jeans), Bill believed that True Fit could become a data analytics platform for the entire apparel industry. Like Pandora for music or Netflix for movies, True Fit aspired to use data to improve the apparel shopping experience. They were already increasing their sales by understanding consumers better. Why couldn't they help much larger organizations do the same thing?

Seen through the lens of the VPM, Bill had a lot of evidence to support the two assumptions we've explored already. Is this a burning problem? Yes, online retailers see painfully low conversion rates in apparel and, worse, a lot of product gets returned. And does the solution uniquely solve the problem? True Fit's algorithms had already shown that they could improve online conversion and lower returns.

The most pressing assumption Bill faced, however, was

whether he and his team were able to deliver the solution. Bill's expanded business model rested on the belief that retailers would share data — buying behavior, consumer information, and sales numbers — with his fledgling firm. What's more, he needed to ensure that he had the analytics expertise to convert all that data — likely in a wide variety of formats from disparate sources — into useful insights. Those are big assumptions, and ones he needed to address right away if this new growth strategy was going to get off the ground.

Fundamentally, this was a question about Bill's team and assets. Or, more precisely, could Bill get the assets (data) and people (expertise) he needed to deliver a solution that his customer (retailers) would love? In the end, he found that he had, or could acquire, the assets he needed. To date, TrueFit has raised more than $150 million and counts dozens of name-brand retailers among its clients.

Like Bill, you and your team need to be able to deliver whatever solution you're proposing. That seems like a simple assumption, but it's one that too few innovators seriously and methodically consider. Delivering isn't merely about getting a product to work; it's about getting it to market consistently, legally, ethically, and profitably.

3.5 Can You Convert Your Customer?

When my team and I met Russell, he had a modest but passionate dream: he wanted to turn the game he'd invented into a thriving family business. The concept he brought us was simple. Two players take turns throwing ping-pong balls into a basket placed several yards away. Each player throws a different colored ball. The basket feeds into seven separate columns. As the ping-pong balls collect in these columns, the first player to line up four of their balls, horizontally, vertically, or at an angle, wins. Russell calls his game Battle Toss.

One of Russell's Battle Toss prototypes.

Russell had come to MAGNET for help with manufacturing. Specifically, he wanted us to design a plastic version of the game that could be produced relatively inexpensively in large quantities. To Russell, plastic seemed like the best material because it enabled mass manufacturing and fast assembly. He also thought that a more durable material like plastic would appeal to his presumed target, college students. He built the prototype (out of wood) in his home woodshop and filed a patent for the game. When he contacted MAGNET, he was waiting for the United States Patent Office examiner to respond. But Russell's vision went well beyond this imperfect wooden contraption. He wanted to build a company that manufactured and sold high-quality games of his own design.

As Russell recounted his journey, he told a familiar story. Sharing his idea mostly among friends and family, he had received rave reviews. "Everyone loves it!" he proudly announced. "Now, I just need to make a lot more of them."

Of course, Russell was making an important assumption. He believed his target (college students) would buy the game. In the Value Proposition Matrix framework, this is the fourth and final foundational assumption — that an innovator can sell their product.

Like each of the foundational assumptions, only evidence derived from real customers, shielded from biases, can demonstrate that someone will pay for a new-to-the-world solution.

The Demand Challenge

Innovators tend to focus on the challenges associated with building their products or delivering their services rather than exploring whether customers will buy what they are creating. In other words, they are relatively overconfident in demand for their product and relatively under-confident in their ability to supply the product.

Here are some common early-stage innovator concerns I encounter:

"I'm looking for a factory and a warehouse."

"I need to build an efficient supply chain."

"How can I make this as cheaply as possible?"

"I need a scale manufacturing partner."

"I want to buy raw material to get the volume discount."

"It has to work perfectly the first time."

"I'm looking for several million dollars in seed funding."

Often these concerns come from innovators who haven't made a single sale. I rarely encounter innovators who express doubt about whether anyone will pay for what they're trying to build or whether what they're building solves an important problem.

This tendency causes all sorts of undesirable outcomes.

Innovators go looking for unrealistic amounts of money and resources. They focus on perfecting *their* version of the initial product rather than considering the *customer's* perfect version. Worse, they might spend money (their own or an investor's) on an idea without any evidence that customers will pay for it.

Even if innovators can resist the temptation to invest in development, capital, or real estate, they often spend a lot of time planning the scale version of their idea. Large companies notoriously fall into this scale planning trap, but startup founders are not immune either. Locked inside their internal product development path, they tend to neglect or entirely ignore what demand dictates.

The diagram below offers a simple way to divide the VPM into Demand and Supply questions:

Can you convert your customer?

DEMAND QUESTIONS

SUPPLY QUESTIONS

Is this a burning problem?

Can you deliver the solution?

Does the solution solve the problem?

Demand questions reside in the upper-left half of the model. They revolve around the customer. Supply questions reside in the lower-right half of the model. They revolve around the solution.

Innovators have a bias toward working on supply questions because the outcomes are relatively controllable. Building solutions and delivering them is often a matter of planning, investing, and executing. This is a space in which most people are more comfortable operating because it doesn't require customers to buy in — it simply requires the physical elements of a product, design of the code, or links in a supply chain to function.

On the other hand, questions of demand are far harder to pin down and are never under an innovator's control. **Whether a customer will pay for a solution or even care about a supposed problem is not something an innovator can fundamentally change. Rather, innovators must discover whether their assumptions about customers are correct and adjust to that reality.** Pinning the viability of a beloved project entirely on customers' whims can be a deeply unsettling notion for an innovator. Yet, that is the foundation of value proposition-focused innovation.

Understanding this inherent bias is not enough. Innovators must actively fight against it by vetting demand questions just as thoroughly as supply questions. The next chapter will unpack some tools and techniques to help make that (often overwhelming) challenge a little less daunting.

Chapter Four
Vetting Demand

Synopsis: Great innovators understand and test their fundamental assumptions, especially those that have to do with demand. Systematically vetting demand assumptions falls into two categories:

Listening to customers
Selling minimum viable products

4.1 Rubber, Meet Road

> *"Plan for what is difficult while it is easy.*
> *Do what is great while it is small."*

— Sun Tzu, Chinese General and Author of *The Art of War*

Thus far, we've explored what could rightly be called "innovation theory." Using only a piece of paper, an innovator could use the Value Proposition Matrix to answer their four core value questions, develop a rough value proposition, and begin to consider the four critical assumptions. But from here, the road gets much steeper. The effort it will take to make progress requires not just hypotheses and plans but action, and not the safe kinds of actions one can accomplish from the cozy confines of an office. The effort required to adequately vet assumptions revolves around pushing ideas (or imperfect representations of them) into the unforgiving maw of the marketplace.

The *Oxford English Dictionary* defines vetting as "the process of checking something with great care." To vet is to methodically root out truths, strengths, and flaws. This is hard work and often intimidates innovators.

To simplify this decidedly uninviting process, let's start by reviewing the two vetting themes that relate to demand questions: *listening* and *selling*.

Here's how this looks when aligned with the VPM framework:

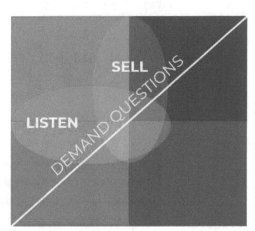

We'll start with listening, the best way to vet the "burning problem" assumption.

4.2 Listening

There are several ways to understand what matters to customers, and they all involve what Steve Blank, entrepreneur, and author, plainly calls "getting out of the building." **You must interact with** your target customers, listen carefully to their stories, and internalize *their* experiences. Here are a few common approaches:

Experience

First, *experience* the problem from your customer's point of view by researching, shopping for, and buying competitive products, then using them the way your target might. Alternatively, this might mean experiencing a competitive service from start to finish. While it's impossible to inhabit the mind of your target, it is important to try by approximating their available alternatives as closely as possible.

Innovators often feel they've already taken this step because their original inspiration came from encountering the problem themselves. While that may be true, it's rarely sufficient. Don't make the mistake of believing you fully understand your target's pains and frustrations just because you count yourself among that group. You are automatically an outlier simply because you've chosen to focus so intently on a problem that others probably see as one of many throughout any given day.

One safe assumption you can always make? Your first experience with a problem isn't representative of your target at large. Experience it anew from as many angles as you can. Canvas the options available through channels, distributors, or stores that you don't usually frequent. Try tools that attempt to solve the problem you're solving but that you're unfamiliar with. Expand your vocabulary by talking with others about the problem, then use those search terms to educate yourself in new, deeper directions. Time and again, I've helped clients unearth products they didn't know existed or services that approximated (or improved upon) their ideas, simply by pushing past what they have seen or experienced so far.

Observation

Observation is a classic technique used in just about every industry, and for good reason. Formalized in frameworks like

Design Thinking, this is the act of watching potential customers and noting pain points (irritation, cost, delays) they encounter. Observation can take place in controlled environments (e.g., recruiting people to undertake specific tasks.) It can also be done "in the wild" by finding people who experience the problem you hope to solve and watching them consider, approach, tackle, and struggle with it. This technique is useful when the assumptive problem is easy to observe. For example, one of my clients was developing a robot to automate roof installations. But, after watching roofers install new roofs, he realized that tearing off the old roof is the most time-consuming and dangerous part of a job. That insight helped him reframe his development efforts on a robot that could automate and expedite removing worn roof shingles.

When creating a new product with American Greetings, the world's second largest greeting card company, I helped an innovation team observe potential early adopters as they interacted with a competitor's website, watching as they explored the pages and made purchasing decisions. We simply sat beside users and observed their journey from first encountering the site to the purchase and confirmation process. This is a frequently used tactic because it helps illuminate the problems consumers experience with alternative solutions. You can see if they struggle with anything right away, from the shopping environment and flow to product assortment and item features.

Some consumer behaviors are particularly useful to note when looking for burning problems. Any sort of "hack" or deliberate workaround using unexpected methods is a good tip-off that this is a problem worth exploring. If a consumer goes to great lengths to assemble their own solution out of disjointed parts, there may well be an opportunity to create a product or service that performs the function of the hack more efficiently. For example, someone who wants to practice their tennis stroke in the winter might rig up a net and make-shift ball return in their basement. That person, in turn, might be willing to pay for a kit designed specifically for indoor, individual tennis practice.

Doing something painful and frustrating again and again is another burning problem tip-off. For example, the founders of Instacart noticed that people would put up with traffic, spotty inventory, and long lines to complete their grocery shopping every week. Offering to have professional shoppers search for and deliver their groceries certainly addressed a burning problem. If a consumer repeatedly fights through a painful experience, that suggests they value the outcome and might pay for a better way to achieve it.

On the other hand, observation isn't ideal for internal (i.e., emotional or mental) pains or frustrations. That's where interviews are useful.

Interviews

One-on-one conversations are another valuable tool in the innovator's toolkit. However, interviews can be fraught with misinformation. For many reasons, people aren't always forthcoming about their views, desires, or intentions.

The key to distilling quality information from interviews with consumers is to carefully structure those conversations. I highly recommend reviewing Gif Constable's, *Talking to Humans* when, well, you plan to talk to humans about the problems you are trying to solve. It's a brisk exploration of how to get useful information from potential customers through observation and interviews. Here is a summary of Constable's key points:

Don't lead conversations toward your solution. Instead, ask questions that allow the person you're interviewing to reveal their thoughts and experiences in the context of the problem you're solving. A great way to do that is to *ask for stories* that include the type or types of problems you're looking to solve. Stories are full of rich information because they are a first-hand account of thoughts, feelings, and actions. These experiences are not hypothetical (what a person might do in a given scenario) but what actually happened. Stories can also be an easier communication vehicle for interviewees. It's intimidating to answer rapid-fire interview questions. Open-ended questions are much more inviting. "Tell me about a time…" or "What was it like when…?" encourage people to open up.

Look for patterns as you gather stories. Because you should be talking to lots of people about their experiences, write down or record what they say. Look for themes that show up again and again. These recurring themes become the basis for addressable insights.

I once worked with a startup that was trying to develop a more aerodynamic wind turbine blade. After a series of customer interviews one of the founders declared, "Our target customer simply isn't trying to solve the problem we thought we were solving." They had talked with half a dozen wind farm owners about the inefficiency of their wind turbines and realized that, as they said, "These folks aren't worried about trying to find a more aerodynamic blade. It seems like what they have is good enough. Convincing them otherwise would take a massive effort." However, an unexpected theme emerged in their conversations. Several of the wind farm operators had complained that the turbine gearboxes failed a lot. From those conversations, my client decided to pivot toward developing sensors that could help predict gearbox failures.

Group conversations, often called focus groups, are another form of interview. While these can be highly efficient at getting lots of consumer reactions in a single discussion, they have limitations. Simply by listening to one another, groups can too often succumb to groupthink. One outgoing or particularly opinionated participant can color the entire discussion. Whenever listening to groups, watch the interpersonal dynamics and follow up with individuals who others might have influenced.

Surveys

Of course, in-person conversations take a lot of time. In some cases, *surveys* can be effective. The rise of digital tools like SurveyMonkey and Google Forms, combined with the long reach of social media sites, has made it easier than ever to cast a wide net for consumer information. However, beware — surveys are easy to overuse and just as easy to misinterpret. They are not generally a great way to assess what consumers will do or how much they are willing to pay.

For obvious reasons, innovators commonly structure surveys to find out what consumers would do in a purely hypothetical situation: "*Would you buy my product? How many would you buy? How often? How much would you pay?*" But, like consumer conversations, survey responses do not contain facts about what consumers will do; they simply reflect what consumers say. Here, again, biases routinely cloud the truth. That is because the difference between what we say we will do and what we do is often vast.

This phenomenon is called Hypothetical Bias — the tendency to misrepresent what we will do when presented with an imaginary scenario. Examples are everywhere. From checking our smart devices less to flossing our teeth more, human beings say they'll do one thing (often what we aspire to do) and do another (often what's easier, cheaper, or more familiar).

Several studies have demonstrated the difference between what a person says they will do when responding to a survey and what they end up doing. One of the most notable (and disturbing) of these studies, titled "Attitudes vs. Actions" was published in 1934 by the Stanford sociologist Richard LePiere. LePiere travelled around the country, visiting more than 250 hotels and restaurants with a Chinese couple. Given the racial prejudices at the time, the participants expected to be turned away from most of these establishments. However, that happened only once. But six months later, when LePiere sent a survey to the places he visited asking whether they would deny serving a person of Chinese descent, 92% of respondents reported they would *not* serve Chinese clientele. In a more contemporary example, Paschal Sheeran found that between half and a quarter of survey respondents who intended to use condoms, get cancer screenings, and exercise, failed to do so. How people respond to new products and services is no different. A 2019 analysis of 77 studies found that people overstate their willingness to pay (the value they report they would pay for a product or service) by 21%.

Hypothetical Bias makes surveying potential customers about their future behaviors a dubious idea. Unfortunately, that is exactly what many innovators end up doing. Time and again, I've seen an entrepreneur present data from a survey that confidently announces, "60% of consumers surveyed would buy this product!" — only to discover that this data was disastrously misleading. (To learn more about the biases that trip innovators up, vist Chapter Seven.)

This is not to say that surveys can't be useful. They can, but **surveys are best deployed to find information on past behaviors or current preferences.** Human beings are better (albeit not perfect) at reporting what they've done than what they will do.

That said, surveys can still be effective tools. For example, I once helped an entrepreneur named Brian quickly kill an early-stage business idea by conducting a simple survey. Brian believed that he could improve the way people give each other books. For hundreds of years, books have been produced and sold in the same way. Giving someone a book used to be simple: go to a bookstore, buy a book, deliver it (sometimes wrapped). There was one way to give a book because people only read books one way.

Today, audiobooks and e-books are becoming increasingly more common, at least in Brian's social circle. Brian and many of his friends frequently listen to audiobooks and read e-books. It seemed to him like a growing trend.

Given the variety of formats, how should one go about giving someone else a book? How would you know what type of book they'd prefer? Brian thought perhaps he could create a platform that would make it easy to give a book and let the recipient choose the format.

To vet his key assumption — in this case, that this was a problem other people experienced — Brian sent out a nine-question survey through his social media channels. He asked book lovers for their thoughts and gathered 35 responses about their past experiences buying books as gifts. This is what he learned: Amazon has made it incredibly easy to buy books as gifts, and easy for gift recipients to return them if they prefer a different format. With a quick canvass, Brian had his answer; his idea simply wasn't addressing a burning problem. Was this approach scientific? No. Was it highly targeted? No. But was it inexpensive and informative enough to point him in another direction? Absolutely.

Research

Another important tool to explore assumptions is research. This includes search engine trends, product reviews, message boards, product FAQs, forums, news articles, and industry reports.

As with all vetting instruments, direct feedback from customers is the most useful. The things consumers are searching for online can be a good indication of the problems they're looking to solve. However, consumers only search for what they know, and figuring out search volumes for "how do I..." entries can be difficult without search engine expertise.

If your idea is related to a current product or service, reviews might offer nuggets of insight. Today, consumers share loads of information about their likes and dislikes online. Using these raves and rants to learn from competitors' successes and failures is inexpensive and highly effective. Low star ratings and consistently negative reviews on competitive or substitute goods or services could suggest that an alternative might better serve a segment of consumers. Stellar reviews might highlight the key attributes of a product or service. With careful study, innovators can reconstruct a lot about how consumers view a market.

Online conversations on large platforms like Facebook, Twitter, Craigslist, and Reddit offer abundant dialogue about problems. More and more, people are turning to the crowd to share, troubleshoot, and commiserate on just about every issue imaginable. Wondering if there's a market for your all-natural horsefly repellent? There's a forum for that:

Horse Fly Problem
Submitted 14 days ago by [withheld]
I recently bought an annual state park pass and have been using it to hike and go to the beach. Unfortunately there is an infestation of horse flies on the trails and it makes hiking unbearable. I bought bug spray with DEET, but that did not work. I tried looking online for a solution but all I found were at-home traps and horses. Does anyone know of a spray or oil or anything that will keep them away while you are hiking?

Reddit, where I found this post within a few seconds of searching for "horsefly problem," has over 1.6 billion monthly visits. It offers a vast collection of topics to explore, each neatly organized into searchable posts and threads. What's more, you can participate in these conversations. Just be careful not to pitch your product — moderators tend to frown on solicitation unless you have explicit permission. Instead, stick to vetting. You'll learn a lot more from listening to your customers than you will from talking at them.

Exploring whether you're addressing a burning problem is not simply revisiting the same Solvable, Scalable, Significant questions we asked in section 2.4. Rather, we're asking whether the problem is important to our target consumer. Instead of looking through a wide-angle lens at the scope and scale of the problem, here you're using a magnifying glass to determine whether a given problem is of particular concern to your early adopters. You can use several (or, better yet, all) of the aforementioned techniques to investigate how your clearly defined customer feels about the problem or problems you suspect they're experiencing.

A note about listening

No matter how you go about listening to your target, understand that interviews are *not* market validation exercises. Again, what people say they *would do* and what they *will do* are two different things. Unfortunately, innovators of all stripes conflate the two, often mistakenly. Done correctly, listening to customers is likely to provide good evidence about their problems. However, regardless of the approach, listening will not provide reliable evidence for or against consumers' willingness to pay for a given solution. **The only way to know if people will pay for something is whether they open their wallets.** This mistake is so common that I consider it a ubiquitous innovation trap to be avoided at all costs.

Listening is best used to understand problems. Next, we will discuss methods better suited to gauging consumer demand.

4.3 Selling

"If you're not embarrassed by the first version of your product, you've launched too late."

— Reid Hoffman, Founder of LinkedIn

Innovators trying to sell their ideas run into a universal entrepreneurial paradox: the best way to assess demand for a product is to try selling it, but how do you make sales if you don't have any product? To solve this, innovators may rush to make the product they've imagined. But how do you know what consumers really want until you show them? How do you afford to build all that product — even if you know exactly what to build — until you have sales revenue?

These challenges aren't new. Innovators often attempt to overcome them by convincing early investors to provide enough seed capital to fund the large-scale development and production of an idea. That's a good approach if the early version of the product turns out to be very close to the one target customers want. But what if the concept is flawed but fixable? Is there a better way to launch a product than simply making as much of it as possible? Is there some way potential customers could help you root out and address those issues without betting years of your life and your retirement savings? There is.

Minimum Viable Products

Bruce Lee said, "Simplicity is the key to brilliance." He knew that in a fight, simple movements not only conserved energy but increased speed. The faster and more efficiently he moved, the greater the advantage over his opponent. While the martial arts icon predated lean innovation by more than three decades, Lee probably would have liked what lean innovation practitioners call the Minimum Viable Product (MVP).

An MVP is a simple (the minimal part) product through which a consumer can signal credible demand (the viable part). In other words, it's a product that's just good enough for a customer to pay for.

Collecting demand signals is a crucial step in the product development journey, a step that, ideally, comes *before* the product is fully developed. Research and interviews simply aren't good enough to assess real-world demand. As discussed, consumers send confusing signals when asked abstract questions like, "Would you buy this hypothetical product?" However, "*Will* you buy this tangible product?" is a far more powerful question. Using an MVP is a way to ask, "Will you?" rather than "Would you?" without building the final product first.

To pull this off, an MVP must have the essential elements that make a product or service unique and useful while still being a work in progress. In other words, customers should be able to buy a functional but unrefined version of the product. By selling this "imperfect," but sound product, an innovator can gauge demand and establish an important check against common biases. What innovators imagine consumers want from their products rarely holds up to reality. Instead, MVPs give innovators invaluable feedback about their products before they've invested more than they should on features their target customers consider unimportant or superfluous. Instead, what customers love or hate about an MVP becomes the product development roadmap.

Like most lean innovation principles, explaining these concepts is straightforward, but using them is harder. In no situation is that felt more acutely than when building an MVP. As we'll see, experimenting with MVPs forces an innovator to strike a delicate, difficult balance between what is *minimal* and what is *viable*.

MVP vs. Prototype

To better frame this concept, it's important to distinguish between an MVP and a prototype. Prototypes help determine whether a product solves the problem it's meant to solve (we will explore this further in Chapter Five). An MVP, on the other hand, demonstrates whether consumers are willing to pay for that solution.

This is a subtle but crucial difference. Getting something to work — for the code to function or the chemistry to react— can be critical to getting early-stage input from potential customers as to whether it solves their problem. But figuring out whether someone will pay for that solution means putting consumers in a position where they can demonstrate credible demand. These are two very different things.

Figuring out whether someone will hand over their credit card isn't the same as understanding whether a product or service delivers what it promises. Sometimes innovators have difficulty separating the two because they believe if their prototype works (i.e., it solves the problem), customers will surely buy it. This isn't necessarily true. Sometimes fundamental issues like high cost, confusing marketing messages, existing processes, or inconvenient sales channels, stand in the way. Sometimes more complex issues emerge. For example, a sale might require an onerous approval process, the customer might have to convince influential stakeholders, or the customer's organization could be particularly resistant to such a change. While a prototype might delight a tester, whether that person becomes a paying customer is a different and distinct line of inquiry.

Of course, there are a lot of ways to vet demand. Established companies might spend years and millions of dollars researching consumer trends, segmenting the market, experimenting with products, optimizing supply chains, marshaling channel partners, and coordinating their marketing efforts, all before selling a single new product. This is called a waterfall or stage-gate process. Each careful step flows into the next as a team follows a pre-set script of activities. Here's an example of that script from a multi-billion-dollar consumer packaged goods company's "product launch playbook":

1. Assemble a cross-disciplinary team from across the organization.
2. Research consumer trends and assess gaps in the current product portfolio.
3. Create a product concept and a business case, including an extensive financial model.
4. Develop a prototype, optimize the manufacturing process, and design an efficient supply chain.
5. Gather product feedback from consumers via surveys, panels, and interviews.
6. Ready the product for commercial release by incorporating consumer feedback, preparing full-scale

production, and finalizing marketing support.

7. Launch nationally across multiple channels and support with advertising.

In this waterfall process, the product development team moves deliberately from one step to the next, building toward a product launch. The expected timeframe from assembling a team to launching the product is between eighteen and twenty-four months. (This might look a lot like the "old way" of working we examined in Chapter One.)

Following that path might well lead to something viable, but there will be nothing minimal about it. If consumers respond favorably, that kind of approach can be a roaring success. If they don't, it will be a terrifically expensive waste of energy, time, and money. Of course, most innovators don't have the resources to develop products this way. Unfortunately, that often doesn't stop them from trying. I've seen innovators spend years "researching" the market and developing a product before exposing their concept to a single consumer. Just as with established company innovation, entrepreneurs who take this path can find success, but they're taking extraordinary—and unnecessary—risks doing so.

Instead, why not embrace the principles of lean innovation and spend as little money and time as possible, learning as much as possible about demand? How much of that long, expensive process can we strip away while still uncovering whether consumers want what we're selling? That's what makes the MVP so compelling.

Great MVPs address specific questions. Will a consumer hit the "buy now" button on a website? Will a corporate buyer place a purchase order after seeing a well-thought-out presentation? Will a pre-order campaign get traction? An MVP should be built around whichever assumption(s) an innovator has identified.

Let's revisit Battle Toss. What Russell thought he wanted as a next step was a large production process, but what he needed was more evidence that consumers would buy his game before he generated a warehouse full of them.

The concept he brought us, despite its handmade feel and cosmetic imperfections, worked rather well. After our first meeting, Russell left the prototype with my team. We had a blast challenging each other to an impromptu Battle Toss tournament. One of my colleagues, overhearing our shouts and laughter, stopped in to play. Ten minutes later, he offered to buy the prototype — he wanted to take it home to play with his kids. In our next meeting with Russell, we shared our experience and made a suggestion: rather than focus on manufacturing, why not develop a dozen or so MVPs — by hand, out of wood — and see if we could sell them? As excited as we were at the prospect, the idea of selling something he'd made by hand terrified Russell.

Almost without exception, physical product entrepreneurs want to make great — if not perfect — products. So, I understand their response when I suggest selling an MVP. "But it's not ready yet!" Or "It's nowhere close to perfect; what if customers hate it?"

This was Russell's response too. "Oh, I don't know," he demurred, "do you really think it's good enough to sell? There are so many things I want to change, and I really think people will want it to be made out of smooth, colorful plastic."

It's natural to want customers to experience the "perfect" version of a product. The things we buy at big-box retailers sure seem perfect, after all. That sends powerful signals to innovators that their products, too, must leap onto shelves in an equally polished form. Thus, because an MVP is, by definition, "minimal," innovators often reject the suggestion...at first.

But, upon further inspection, how foreign is the MVP concept really? **Consumers buy "imperfect" or experimental products all the time.** Diners regularly order a chef's nightly special, which is often an experimental menu item. Tech enthusiasts enthusiastically pre-order the latest gadget, knowing the early version will likely include some bugs. Farmers' Market patrons will buy foods and cosmetics that have been made, packaged, and labeled by hand. Deal-seekers will buy all types of used items, from furniture and clothing to kitchen gadgets and yard equipment. Yes, when we walk into a sporting goods store, we expect that pair of yoga pants or a package of golf balls to deliver a fresh-from-the-factory feel. But that's not the case for countless exchanges.

By realizing that consumers are often willing to buy things that aren't "flawless," innovators can free themselves from the mistaken belief that they need to perfect their product or service before selling it.

In fact, the very notion of conceiving, developing, and commercializing a product that flawlessly meets the market's needs is an entrepreneurial pipe dream. Even within the stage-gate process, developing a useful, viable product requires consumer interaction and feedback. An MVP is simply another way to gather feedback, but with the necessary gravity that monetary exchange creates.

It's also important to note that the MVP relies on the idea that consumers are willing to look past imperfections in the hopes of solving a particular problem. This reinforces the concept of targeting early adopters by identifying their burning problems. If the problem at the heart of a value proposition is truly a burning one, early adopters won't hold innovators trying to solve said problem to exceedingly high standards. Rather, early adopters will likely consider (and sometimes purchase) any attempt to address that problem.

Imagining how an innovator might sell a product to early adopters without reaching the high bar of "perfect" opens numerous pathways to gauge market demand. We'll explore several below.

NOTE: While I encourage innovators to lower the high bar on their product development efforts, there is a crucial caveat: MVPs should always be safe and legal. Never offer consumers an experimental product or service that hasn't been properly designed to ensure the user's safety or doesn't meet applicable legal and regulatory standards. Sometimes getting these assurances is a matter of opinion, and I cannot tell you where the "safe" and "legal" threshold is for every product. But do not cut corners when it comes to either of these areas. MVPs are designed to help innovators move faster and learn more, but that must never come at the expense of consumer safety or put anyone at legal risk.

Selling an MVP

As consumers search for, research, and buy products, they're sending signals about their interest levels and purchase intent. Companies use this data to better understand the demand for and relative success of their products — from a passing interest to a repeat purchase — and can glean even more insights thanks to reviews, recommendations, and referrals.

Luckily, innovators can use the same information to test their assumptions without over-investing in product development. Here are some examples:

Ad response

In 1704, a property owner paid the *Boston News-Letter* to announce that an Oyster Bay, Long Island estate was for sale. "There is a very good Fulling-Mill to be let or sold ... Enquire of Mr. William Bradford, Printer in New York, and know further." In the 300 years since then, advertisers have been following a remarkably similar formula to generate demand for products and services: inform a target market (in this case, readers of the *Boston News-Letter*) that a product (a lovely Oyster Bay development) is available for sale, then encourage prospective buyers with a call-to-action (talk to Mr. Bradford).

Compare that to a modern-day ad from ESPN.com: "The ESPN Daily, Get the best of ESPN sent to your inbox," with a "Sign me up!" button to click. The same basic structure applies; a target (ESPN readers), an offer (a digital newsletter), and a call-to-action (Sign up!).

Whether the consumer is a would-be 18th Century landowner or a current-day sports enthusiast, the signals they send by stopping in or clicking are essentially the same; they're interested in the product being advertised.

These demand signals give sellers invaluable information about a buyer's interest. Inquiries (or their modern equivalent, clicks) represent a form of intent — basically an assertion that says the product on offer is, at least in part, compelling. The number of people who respond to a property ad or click on a digital banner provides a measure of evidence that the product is resonating with interested buyers.

Yes, you can also simply ask consumers if they're interested. But consider how an ad response differs from, say, a focus group. In a focus group, pre-selected consumers are prompted with extensive information about a product, then invited to imagine how they might respond if that product were offered to them. On the other hand, ads invite consumers, stopped in the natural course of their day, to act based on their level of interest in a simple offer. The former is a synthetic exercise, fraught with bias. The latter activates a part of the sales cycle.

When it comes to MVPs, ads are powerful tools. Ads can be simple MVPs themselves because they require almost no product development but present a viable value proposition.

Imagine an ad that reads, "Check out this amazing new product!" then directs interested consumers to a website that reads, "Thanks for checking us out. This product is coming soon!" That ad is testing demand without having to have the product ready to sell. Better yet, in a digital world, ads can be targeted directly to early adopters based on their digital profile or browsing habits.

But wait, is it ethical to advertise a product that isn't ready to sell? I believe it is, so long as the ad doesn't indicate the product is available, and the purchase path (or lack thereof) makes it clear that the concept is in development. For example, showing a picture of a concept product and saying, "Buy this now!" would be misleading at best and false advertising at worst. However, it's common and perfectly acceptable to show that same picture and say, "Learn more!" or "Check this out!" The next thing a consumer sees — ideally a website or comprehensive landing page — should immediately clarify that the product is still under development.

Crowdfunding sites like Kickstarter market unfinished, in-development, or beta-stage products as a feature, not a bug, of their platform. Those who frequent Kickstarter understand that their orders might not immediately convert into a delivery (if at all). In exchange, these consumers get to see (and hopefully experience) cutting-edge technology and design. The risk that the product fails before it makes it to market or is less-than-perfect once it arrives is outweighed by the possibility that it could finally solve a vexing problem.

There are many ways to advertise MVPs. One of the most useful is posting or buying ad space on social media platforms like Facebook, LinkedIn, or YouTube. It can also be highly effective to buy search terms related to the concept from search engines like Google, then direct clicks to a simple landing page. Both approaches can be inexpensive and effective when executed well. However, be aware that taking either path is best done with the assistance of a professional. The intricacies of search and social advertising can seem simple but often turn out to be complex and time-consuming to do right.

Traditional ad vehicles like print, direct mail, and radio can also be effective. These, too, can drive consumers to a website or a phone number for more information.

No matter the channel, however, it's critical to measure the response and, if possible, engage interested early adopters. To do that, you will need to gather information about them.

Information exchange

The classic information exchange scenario is for the seller to incentivize consumers to share their information by offering something "extra." Whether that's more detail about a concept, advanced notice of a product launch, the chance to try a prototype, or early access to a beta test or pilot experience. All that is required of the potential customer is their contact information and perhaps a bit more about who they are and why they are interested in the product.

We've all visited websites that require us to provide personal information — name, email, address, date of birth, etc. — before going any further. Most consumers pause at that moment and do some mental math. Is the information behind this "wall" worth the personal details the site requests? Where will that data go, who will see it, how will it be used? Perhaps it'll add spam email to their inbox, but there's always a chance that it could lead to more meddlesome or nefarious issues, like identity theft. In a world where sharing personal data can be costly, the mere fact that consumers are willing to do so indicates they see value in the exchange.

While sharing data isn't as indisputable a demand signal as spending money, it is a demand signal, nevertheless. Therefore, innovators can use information exchange as evidence in support of (or against) their value proposition hypothesis.

Dropbox, a file-sharing software platform, did this with tremendous success well before their first complete product was even functional. In the early days of development, Dropbox's founder, Drew Houston, made a simple video explaining how his product would allow files from one device to be shared seamlessly across other devices. While this mock demo was a concept only, hundreds of thousands of people signed up for the Dropbox beta waiting list. According to Houston, that list went from 5,000 people to 75,0000 "literally overnight."

While this waiting list wasn't full of paying customers, these were people willing to share their information with Dropbox in exchange for a chance to test the product. That simple demand signal turned out to be a strong indication of things to come. As of 2021, Dropbox is valued at more than $8.8 billion.

Pre-orders

Of course, names and email addresses don't represent tangible demand; they merely signal that demand. Orders represent demand. But if your MVP isn't ready to ship, deliver, or launch, try taking pre-orders.

In 2016, a technology company called Remarkable did just that. The Norwegian startup had developed what might seem a decidedly un-remarkable product — a tablet. As Android and Apple tablets were flooding the market, it was hard to see how a small tablet with no brand recognition would stand out. Almost unbelievably, the product didn't even connect to the internet.

However, the Remarkable team was making a bold assumption built on a simple insight — that people who prefer to write on paper with a pen could be converted to a digital tablet that feels like working on paper.

To test this assumption, they produced a video that beautifully and simply showed their product in action. "Paper is the ultimate tool for thinking," the narrator explains, "but if you love paper, you probably struggle to keep track of your notebooks." It was aimed at people who enjoy the tactile feel of a pen scratching on paper but wanted the convenience of digital records. The technology looked believable, and the value proposition hit home for their target, "the paper person," their ad claimed.

The video offered a simple nudge to visit their site, remarkable.com, where excited "paper people" would find the message that the company was taking a limited number of pre-orders, with a delivery date six months in the future.

This pre-order path isn't all that unique, but it fits neatly into the VPM framework. The Remarkable team believed they were solving an important problem, that paper was hard to manage, but digital substitutes didn't offer the right feel. They also believed their paper-like digital writing surface would solve the problem. Lastly, they put themselves in a position to deliver the product. They simply needed orders to address the critical assumption that they could convert "paper people." But rather than over-investing in the product, messaging, or channels, first they chose to invest a little money in a video and a website. This allowed them to take orders in batches, offering early adopters willing to wait half a year the chance to buy the product. Those pre-orders—tens of thousands of them—provided enough evidence and capital to lean into their concept and build out their full production capability.

Joint Development Agreements

Developing most products is expensive, but building products that require complex engineering can be *very* expensive. That's doubly true for energy systems. So, it didn't come as a surprise when Dave, a new client, explained that his project, a drone power system that could vastly increase a drone's flight time, was running out of money.

What he needed, he said, was proof that customers would buy drones equipped with his system. Rather, that's what his potential investors said they needed. They wanted to make sure that at least one customer cared enough about increasing their drones' flight endurance that they would pay for a pricey system. In other words, Dave's investors wanted to know if he could convert a customer.

The problem, of course, was that Dave's prototype wasn't ready. That would take a few hundred thousand dollars. Stuck in a chicken-or-egg paradox, Dave asked for MAGNET's help.

I connected Dave with Jeff Sinclair, a 30-year veteran and Senior Partner at McKinsey & Co., now a teacher of entrepreneurship at the University of Michigan, and an experienced angel investor and advisor, including with drone companies.

Jeff's simple advice was right out of the lean innovation playbook. "You need to get a Joint Development Agreement. If you get a manufacturer and a customer to commit their time, talent (and, ideally, money) to turn your project into a working product, it'll give investors a lot more confidence."

Jeff went on to explain that he'd used these types of agreements to get other tech companies out of similar paradox pits. The MVP, in this case, is the technology and a clear value proposition. Dave promised epic flight endurance. Thus, he needed to find a drone manufacturer, and ideally one of their customers, that cared deeply about extending the flight time of their fleet.

While this isn't a sale, it is decidedly a form of value exchange. People and time are expensive. Good companies don't spend either without believing the investment has merit. A formal agreement that gets key players in the value chain on board can be the validation investors need. That was true in Dave's case. A joint agreement he eventually formed was enough to convince several investors to fund his project. Later, Dave received a multi-million dollar order to develop and deliver units to the US military. That order was thanks in no small part to the development partnerships he had built.

Not every product has a value chain exactly like Dave's, but most innovators have key partners whose buy-in could lend a lot of credibility to their project. Retailers, wholesalers, and even suppliers might have strong customer relationships that put them in a position to see downstream demand. From that vantage point, they may be able to spot the value in innovative but incomplete products. For example, a large grocer might see a rising food trend and be keenly interested in testing it in a handful of stores. An entrepreneur on the cutting edge of that trend might have luck partnering with this chain to fund production and establish credible evidence of demand. Look for ways that these kinds of stakeholders can provide indications of downstream demand.

One note of caution: do not be fooled into thinking that a

downstream partner's interest, excitement, or general encouragement is the same as a joint development agreement. The latter is a legal document outlining how two or more parties will devote resources to a project. The former is very nice to hear. Simply offering encouragement is nothing more than a way for a partner to weigh in without taking any risk. If the project comes to fruition, that partner still stands to benefit. If not, they have risked nothing. Unfortunately, innovators are often duped into thinking that hollow enthusiasm is a legitimate demand signal. Agreements are useful signals. Indicating interest without investment or risk in some form is just hot air.

Try-and-buy

In a world where seemingly everything is connected to the internet, it might be surprising to learn that more than 80% of small- and medium-sized manufacturers in Northeast Ohio (one of the nation's foremost manufacturing regions) do not have a single machine monitored by internet-enabled sensors. Two entrepreneurs, Prince and Lucas, believed they could change that. Using a combination of widely available hardware combined with custom algorithms, they developed a sensor system that could be easily connected to machines in manufacturing settings to detect and interpret vibrations. With this system, even the most technologically unsophisticated manufacturer could analyze factory-floor performance and leverage those insights to make smarter management decisions.

But Prince and Lucas ran into a problem. Many of the manufacturers they approached didn't want to pay for their technology. In many cases, their target customer wasn't internet-enabled, they simply didn't see value in being connected. Recording machine up-time and down-time (when machines are running and not running) could easily be done the way they'd always done it, by recording it on the greasy pads of paper they'd always used.

While Prince and Lucas found a few early adopters that

helped them improve and refine their technology, they needed a new plan if they were going to get market traction. That's when they adopted a try-and-buy approach. They offered to install their technology and share the information they gathered at no charge. All they required was the factory owner or management team's approval and their time to review the findings. If, at the end of the project, the manufacturer still saw no value in the technology, they would pack it up and leave. If this happened enough times, Prince and Lucas knew they would need to pivot. However, that's not what happened. Instead, manufacturer after manufacturer asked them to keep their devices installed and offered to pay them recurring service fees to monitor them and provide analytic insights. Eventually, this approach helped Prince and Lucas earn admission to one of the most prestigious incubators in the world, Y-Combinator.

This is the crucial question in the try-and-buy approach: if an early adopter experiences the MVP, will it be enough to convince them to purchase it? If not, the reasons they give for opting out will feed better, more informed product development. If, however, the test run generates sales, it's evidence that there is, in fact, a market for the product.

Sales

> *"Get out there and try selling the thing!"*
> — Jeff Glueck, former CEO of Foursquare

There is no better evidence of demand than, well, demand. That's obvious. But of all the other methods we've discussed, this is the one that innovators fear the most. Worse, they often believe that other forms of validation can adequately substitute for sales. Or they treat indications of potential sales like demand and invest their energy accordingly.

All the research, fact-finding, competition assessing, customer interviewing, modeling, or prototyping combined is less powerful than one honest sale to a willing and eager buyer.

That is because it is unequivocal proof that someone is willing to part with their money for the product. The price, channel, branding, and promotion, even the product itself, might need to be altered to capture a broader market. But that one spark is the difference between guessing and knowing that a value proposition has genuine merit. While it might seem inconsequential, the gap between zero sales and one sale is far larger than the gap between one and two, or two and one hundred.

Thus, my goal with clients and students is to blaze the shortest path possible to that first sale. Often this is still an arduous process. But shifting the mindset of an innovator from "creator" to "seller" helps illuminate a concrete set of steps, albeit much scarier steps than they're expecting (or willing) to take.

That's because making a sale can, rightly, seem terrifying. What if the product doesn't work? What if the customer hates it? What if nobody wants to buy it at all?

These are menacing questions. But no matter how frightening they are, innovators must eventually face them if they are ever going to turn their idea into a business. The sooner they do, the less likely they are to invest in the wrong path. Translation: **the sooner a viable version of the product is offered for sale, the sooner the real learning begins.**

Of course, if the product truly isn't viable (meaning it doesn't have the core elements and functionality to deliver an approximation of the value proposition), then my advice is to keep working on it until it is. But innovators usually spend too much time tinkering before they finally attempt to make a sale.

Time and again, I've seen that painful, reluctant turning point yield terrifically important insights. More than a few times, I've seen early sales make it clear that the product required massive changes. I've seen promotional messages fly and flop. I've seen the hardest and most necessary outcome — no demand at all — shock innovators into a long-delayed but necessary pivot.

Mike Tyson said, "Everyone has a plan until they get hit for the first time." Likewise, every innovator has a plan until the market pushes back. Nobody said innovation would be easy or pleasant, and getting that first sale is no exception.

Get out there and sell that MVP.

Chapter Five
Vetting Supply

Synopsis: As in vetting demand assumptions, there are a series of critical activities involved in vetting supply assumptions. They fall into two categories:

Building prototypes
Organizing a team and resources

"I made 5,127 prototypes of my vacuum before I got it right. There were 5,126 failures. But I learned from each one."
— Sir James Dyson, Inventor of the Dyson vacuum

"Great things in business are never done by one person. They're done by a team of people."
— Steve Jobs

5.1 The "Easy" Side of the VPM

Let me be clear: there is *nothing* easy about building a business. But when compared with understanding consumer problems and making sales (i.e. exploring demand assumptions), innovators tend to be more comfortable working on designs, solving engineering problems, establishing processes, building financial models, negotiating contracts, finding partners, recruiting a team, or raising money. In other words, innovators tend to embrace developing, creating, coordinating, and launching their ideas and, comparatively, dread exploring whether the market has any use for their ideas. I believe that's because innovators feel they have a direct influence over the outcomes involved in building and organizing — the two key activities required to vet supply-related assumptions.

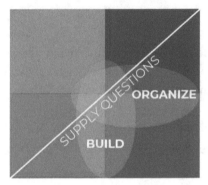

Unlike demand-side assumptions, which put an innovator entirely at the mercy of the market, supply-side assumptions can feel like they fall more under the innovator's control, as they rely on planning and executing, rather than exploring and reacting. Innovators can imagine a product or service and outline the things they need to do to build it. Likewise, they can typically identify the assets they need and acquire them. However, as we'll see, vetting these supply-side assumptions requires plenty of experimentation and flexibility, and getting these assumptions wrong can be no less fatal to a business.

5.2 Building

Building is, as you may recall, about assessing one of the critical assumptions: whether a solution uniquely solves a problem. There are several ways to go about "building." Here are a few of the best.

Benchmarking

Building things is expensive and time-consuming. When looking for evidence that your idea solves a problem, it's often helpful and cost-effective to start by understanding similar products or services. Benchmarking is a way to scan similar technologies, processes, or platforms for the sorts of characteristics or capabilities you hope to employ in your unique solution. It's rare that pieces and parts of a new product or service don't already exist, in some form, somewhere.

My team at MAGNET worked with one entrepreneur, Austin, who believed he could buy second-hand automotive parts in bulk — millions and millions of them — and use automation to sort these jumbled messes into sets. Doing this by hand as a hobby, he had sold second-hand sets at a significant markup, especially those that were rare or discontinued.

Before helping Austin design a mechanized version of this process, we thought about how existing tools and processes might help solve the problem. First, we looked at systems that scan and spot variations in high-volume manufacturing environments to understand if any could identify different sizes, shapes, and colors Then we researched sorting machines commonly used in agriculture. This gave us a good idea of how — once we distinguished between lots of random parts — we could sort them into categories. Finally, we talked to experts who developed cataloguing algorithms to determine if a machine could help keep track of random parts and look for ways to assemble them into high-value sets. Combining this research, we were able to piece together a well-informed picture of whether the hypothetical solution would work using current technology. Ultimately, the technology required to perform this complex sorting operation was too expensive and unreliable for Austin's purposes. But thanks to our benchmarking exercise, he saved a lot of time and money to put toward his next venture.

Benchmarking can be used in virtually any industry. Take

software. There are countless digital analogs for just about any idea. Using analogies like "the Uber" of this, or "the Airbnb" of that, is a useful way to explain a business model, but it can also be helpful to understand the pre-existing platforms and services upon which you may build your idea. (Of course, I am not suggesting that you blatantly copy or recreate someone else's platform.)

The key is to make a thorough inventory of the businesses, processes, products, and technologies that relate to or look like your idea, particularly those that could be repurposed or reimagined to help you build a novel product or service.

Prototyping

Sometimes called a proof-of-concept, a prototype is an attempt to demonstrate that an idea works. This calls to mind the well-worn image of an inventor in a garage soldering, welding, mixing, or coding their idea into existence. In a service business, this can look like an early effort to do work for prospective clients. For example, suppose a company plans to deliver lunches to a daycare (saving parents the hassle of packing lunches and daycares the pain of maintaining an on-site kitchen). As a prototype of the service, the innovator might recruit a few early clients, take orders manually, and make and deliver lunches by hand. In either case, the most important aspect of prototyping is assessing whether and to what extent the solution uniquely solves the target's problem.

When an entrepreneur named Mike reached out to me to talk about his idea for improving mulch, I was intrigued. Mulch isn't a hot category for innovation. Yet, the problems Mike described were readily apparent to anyone who had ever bought, transported, or spread mulch. Moving shredded wood around isn't fun. Just a few bags of mulch will fill the average car's trunk and leave piles of debris behind. And lugging wet, bulky bags is a messy business. "It should be sold with pain killers," Mike jokes. Mulching involves all sorts of painful problems.

Mike started telling me about his solution, which he called Smart Mulch. He described thin, compact, dry tiles of mulch that could be picked up, transported, and placed easily. Once watered, they would break apart and expand into a beautiful, even layer of mulch. His research had already shown that the problem he saw was real, particularly for the owners of homes with smaller plant and flower beds. However, he had yet to show that mulch could be compressed into tiles, much less that it would spring back to its lush former self with a good soaking from a garden hose.

Mike needed to make a prototype.

Using a series of industrial presses that he borrowed, Mike began compressing various types of mulch. He made his first tile using a 10-ton press, producing a two-inch-by-two-inch square that stood nearly as tall as it did wide. Crumbling and small, it wasn't much to look at, but it was enough to test how well it would hold up and, importantly, whether applying water would induce it to expand. It worked, at least in an initial application. Dozens of iterations and larger presses later, Mike produced an 8-inch-by-8-inch tile that stood just over half an inch tall. Not only could it be handled without crumbling, but it would also expand beautifully after a few minutes of watering.

Mike's story is simple but important. While not all ideas need a physical proof-of-concept, it was the right step for him and a good use of resources. If your idea is so new or different that it's unclear whether it will work, consider building a prototype first. Can a roofing robot navigate a rooftop, find old shingles, and strip them off? Does the specialized apparel you've designed fit and function for your customer as you imagined it would? Does your chemistry get marijuana resin off hands and tools? **Build a simple form of your idea. See if it works. Adjust if it doesn't.**

There are facilities all over the world designed to help innovators prototype their ideas. On one end of the spectrum, governments, universities, and companies pump billions of dollars into Research & Development labs. On the other end, inventors tinker and test gadgets in their basements and garages. In the last decade, maker spaces have given innovators access to small-scale manufacturing technologies formerly available only in industrial workshops and laboratories. One of the largest open-to-the-public maker spaces in the world, the Sears think[-box] is part of Case Western Reserve University, where I teach. This seven-story building boasts 50,000 square feet of space. It offers community access to 3D printers and scanners, laser cutters, electronics fabrication stations, industrial sewing machines, design software, a waterjet cutter, welding equipment, CNC mills and lathes, and much more.

However, whether a prototype works is often a subjective assessment. For new products and services, "working" isn't just doing the job — it's doing the job better than existing alternatives.

Controlled testing

Evidence-based innovation puts a high emphasis on getting consumer feedback but it's worth mentioning an important step on the path toward "getting out of the building." Sometimes it's useful to invite consumers "into the building" to provide feedback. The early versions of any product or service will inevitably be warty and buggy. Inviting a cohort of early testers to experience the lab or concept version of a product or service can help expose these problems quickly and systematically, rather than waiting for broader market feedback. This might sound like a simple step, and it certainly can be. Unfortunately, it can also be a hazard for two reasons. First, innovators often over-control their controlled testing. Second, they can spend too much time in a controlled test cycle.

Over-controlling a test comes in many forms. Innovators "lead the witness" as they guide consumers through a process or application. While some instruction might be necessary, it's easy to overdo it or step in and rescue the tester when the test isn't going well. Innovators might also over-control a test by selecting testers already intimately familiar with the product or service or are predisposed not to provide honest feedback (think, your mom or best friend).

Likewise, it's easy to spend too much time in a controlled environment because it's comfortable and safe. But it should be the opposite: brief and brutally honest.

In both cases, the best approach is to (1) recruit unbiased testers, (2) provide only as much instruction or guidance as would be provided if they had encountered the product on their own, then (3) back off and observe.

Occasionally it's appropriate to provide use-cases for testers. These are essentially scripts that list a set of tasks to be accomplished. For example, "Use the app to make a transaction" or "assemble the product." Note that these don't include too many instructions. You want your testers to find the rough edges that real-world users will find. Overly prescriptive steps may hide those pitfalls. While it might not be fun to see your testers struggle, you want to root out those struggles in a low-risk environment.

Look for "show-stoppers" — issues that would keep the product or service from delivering on its core value. Examples include elements that repeatedly break or fail, situations that aggravate users and/or prevent them from using the product or engaging with the service, unenthusiastic responses to the product, or an unwillingness to recommend it to a friend or colleague. Address those, perhaps run another controlled test, *then move on*. Again, resist the urge to "perfect" your product here. It's tempting to stay in the cozy confines of the "lab." Get out into the field and test.

Field testing

Once you've watched your prototype at work in the lab, it's time to relinquish control. Give it to folks in your target niche, ask them to use it however they want, and collect their thoughts.

"Wait," you might be thinking, "if I give this ugly, imperfect prototype to customers, they'll tell me it's ugly and imperfect." Yes, they might. But that's an important part of evidence-based entrepreneurship.

As Steve Blank says, "there are no facts inside the building." **You may think you know how to make a perfect product. You may believe it down to your bones. But you can't know for sure. Do you know who does know? Your customers.**

Innovators make progress by building products and collecting feedback from actual customers, even if that means showing customers something that you think is perhaps too flawed. In the end, you may be surprised at how much better your product will be because of it.

Running a field test

Field tests take planning. Here are some tips to help make the effort a little less daunting:

1. **Know what you want to learn.** Field tests aren't going to go perfectly. Identify the known imperfections and expect those to fall short of expectations. Focus on the core of the product or experience you're creating and the feedback it gets.

2. **Set expectations.** Tell your testers that they're among the first to use your product or service. Make sure they know that their honest feedback is crucial, but also explain that they're likely to encounter bugs and flaws. Ask them to search these out aggressively. There's no bad feedback other than, "It works just fine." Also, make it clear that you're going to be following up for details.

3. **Don't meddle.** While you want to prepare testers with these key pieces of information, you also don't want to guide their experience. Don't walk testers through the user journey; let them experience it on their own. Don't qualify the prototype or apologize about its condition. Let your target use it and watch what happens.

4. **Follow-up and listen carefully.** This may seem like a throwaway tip but following up isn't just about asking how it went. Ask for the full picture, preferably through a story, by asking open-ended questions like "How was your experience?" Listen with an open mind. Don't lead the conversation. Resist the urge to explain why their experience wasn't great ("Oh, that's not ready yet," or "We know that's an issue.") Testers' insights are gold; mine them carefully and learn as much as you can. In-person is always best, but email and survey responses are acceptable if there's no good way to engage face to face.

5. **Take great notes.** Take good, thorough notes or, if you can, record the conversation. Invite a teammate or friend along and compare notes afterward.

5.3 Organizing

Recall the assumption that connects your Team and their associated assets to the unique Solution — that is, that your team can deliver. Vetting this assumption is, at its heart, about getting organized. To deliver consistently, you will need to marshal the right resources—talent, capital, and information—and assemble them in a way that allows you to fulfill your value proposition again and again.

It's easy to get carried away building the "perfect" team. But without stopping to ask critical questions about the state of those assets in the context of the unique solution you're offering to the market, you risk falling into some traps. To help you avoid those, here's a get-organized hit list:

- Scout the competition
- Define the relationship (DTR)
- Sketch a rough P&L
- Identify your key sources of capital

- Assess the IP landscape
- Activate your network
- Get some advisors

Scout the competition

As we've explored, innovators don't always spend enough time identifying and investigating their competition. I blame several phenomena for this surprisingly common blind spot.

First, (as imprudent as this might sound) deep down, we don't want others to have come up with our grand idea, so we often don't look for competing ideas as hard as we should. This is a mirror image of confirmation bias that I'll talk about more about in Chapter Seven. Instead of looking for information to confirm our assumptions, we unconsciously neglect to seek information that discounts (or contradicts) our assumptions.

Second, as we experience problems and don't see immediate solutions, we quickly surmise that good solutions don't exist. This is the availability bias at work (also discussed Chapter 7). In an age when we feel like we can become experts on almost any topic after a few hours on Google, innovators sometimes don't dig much deeper than that.

The good news is that there are many tools to help understand the competition, and the Internet offers an abundance of cheap, powerful ways to gather useful information quickly. (Yes, Google is on that list). Visit lots of different websites. Check out retail stores (yes, in person). Call up competitors' sales or customer service reps. Try their products for yourself if you can. Talk to their users with an open mind. Immerse yourself in understanding the pros and cons of each. Identify the types of consumers that will love the competition and those whose problems remain unaddressed.

There's no single "right way" to learn about market alternatives. However, you must *learn about them*. The first step is accepting that your idea is likely not as unique as you think and expecting to find competitors. If you don't, that's probably a bad sign. There are billions of people in the world and very little pure novelty. If you find yourself alone in what you think is a competition-free space, beware. You're either not looking hard enough, don't fully understand the marketplace, or (and this is key) the market simply isn't there for your product or service.

That said, don't despair in the face of competition either; rather, see it as a healthy sign of demand. Listen to consumers and look for the nuances and subtle differences that could help you create something specifically for an unhappy or underserved segment.

Define The Relationship

DTR stands for Define the Relationship. More specifically, define the relationships that make up your fledgling organization. When you're starting out, you'll likely get help from partners, co-founders, advisors, experts, investors, and many others. Clearly defining the role of each player is a critical step in the process of organizing. It's often said that a co-founder relationship is like a marriage and can be more complicated to maintain, repair, or dissolve. Likewise, the people who support you often aren't doing it out of a purely altruistic desire to help. Sure, family or close friends may pitch in without strings attached (or so it seems), as will a well-meaning advisor. But deep, committed effort — precisely the kind that gets new ventures off the ground — comes with expectations, typically of compensation. Talk about these expectations early and openly. Setting up a formal operating agreement is often a wise step, as is writing down each team member's roles and responsibilities.

Sketch a rough P&L

Whether you're setting up your first lemonade stand or running a billion-dollar company, every business is built on the same simple equation: revenue minus costs equals profit.

A Profit & Loss statement (P&L) is the standard method of laying out that equation, whether real or speculative. The imagined kind is sometimes referred to as a "pro forma" P&L.

Basically, it's a document full of guesses about how much revenue a venture will generate, what it will cost to generate that revenue, and what profit (if any) will be leftover.

I won't cover every aspect of creating a P&L; there are myriad texts and online resources that will do a better and more thorough job than I ever could. But I will point out some of the basic pieces of a P&L and how assembling them thoughtfully can provide an innovator with powerful insights.

Rather than thinking of a P&L as a tool to calculate profits, think about it as a blueprint that describes how a business is designed to function. While the sales and expenses shown on a pro forma are estimates, how those numbers fit together creates a complete picture of how a new venture is supposed to create value.

For example, say an innovator is starting a digital media company all about beer. It includes a plan to launch a blog covering the industry, a podcast exploring the art of homebrewing, and a YouTube channel about gastropubs worldwide. Creating a Pro Forma (while not nearly as fun as international gastropub hopping) is a great way to answer some important structural questions about the plan to earn money (revenue) and what sorts of investments will be required to make that money (costs.)

Revenue could come in many forms, from sponsored airtime on the Podcast, to affiliate marketing (basically paid referrals) on the blog. Each of these revenue streams will have its own line on the P&L. Maybe they look something like this:

Revenue	$350,000
Sponsorships	$300,000
Affiliate referrals	$50,000

But where did those numbers come from? Answering that question (How many sponsors? How much will they pay? How many affiliate referrals? How much per referral?) illuminates a whole series of assumptions about the business. Each assumption is a piece of the bigger picture, and each one has important implications for success or failure.

Exactly how detailed does a Pro Forma need to be? There's no single answer to that question; every Pro Forma is as unique as the business model it describes. However, a P&L should back up the basic pieces with logical assumptions.

Using the example above:

Revenue	$350,000
Sponsorships	$300,000
3 sponsors per podcast	
$5,000 per sponsor	
20 shows	
Affiliate referrals	$50,000
	500,000 clicks
5% of clicks result in a sale	
$50 per sale to affiliate partner	
4% affiliate fee per sale (to us)	

While the mechanisms must make sense (are affiliate referrals really paid this way?), the numbers should also be realistic. Is it reasonable to expect this many sponsors? Will sponsors pay that much per show? Could they pay more? What about the differences among affiliate click rates? Do you have any evidence supporting these assumptions?

Like revenue, outlining costs is also a crucial exercise. Generating revenue takes effort and assets, both of which cost money. These costs are typically divided into two basic categories: fixed (meaning costs that stay the same no matter how many units you produce) and variable (costs that increase proportionately to the number of units produced).

What resources and expertise does it take to produce those podcasts? What capital is required? What about employees or freelancers? Or advertising to generate an audience? Maybe a sales team to find and manage sponsors?

Answers to these questions are built on the types of assumptions outlined in this book. A basic Pro Forma will clarify the levers that make those assumptions work and help pinpoint where they might fail.

Assess the IP landscape

Intellectual Property (IP) is the category of assets that includes patents, copyrights, and trademarks related to creative works like inventions or content. Theoretically, owning these assets gives you the sole right to profit from them, whether through production or licensing. Having exclusive access to IP effectively gives the owner a legal monopoly on a product, and that's why it can be a powerful asset for anyone trying to create a business.

Of course, owning IP doesn't guarantee a smooth path to success. Just because your team owns a patent or copyright doesn't mean that it's valuable. Countless patents have been filed and granted, only to languish without ever finding commercial success.

Even if you successfully commercialize your IP, people infringe on intellectual property rights, knowingly or unknowingly, all the time. When they do, they're liable to get sued. Between 4,000 and 6,000 patent infringement cases are filed in the US each year.

That's why it's critically important to know who owns IP related to your idea, where you and your competitors are free to operate without infringing on anyone's ownership, and when you might want to protect your IP.

This is where I'll make an obligatory disclaimer: **I recommend talking to a knowledgeable IP lawyer when seriously exploring IP and patents.** But before you take that (often costly) step, there are several readily accessible resources to help jump-start your exploration.

Using the United States Patent & Trademark Office (USPTO) website (uspto.gov), you can search a database of more than 200 years' worth of patents filed in the United States.

Google Patents (https://patents.google.com/) also indexes

87 million patents and patent applications from 17 patent offices, including the US, Europe, and China.

Before diving in, I suggest researching how to assess patent claims, which are the most meaningful part of a patent.

While no amount of diligence can ensure that you won't encounter IP issues, infringing on someone's IP or failing to protect your own can be a crippling mistake.

Identify your key sources of capital

Usually, when we talk about an innovator's capital, we think of money, specifically investment dollars. It might also call to mind physical assets. But the concept of capital is broader than that. The wealth of assets that an innovator has goes well beyond cash, machinery, and inventory. Understanding the wider categories of capital — each of which I've briefly described herein — will help you see the unique combination of resources *you* bring to your innovation effort, and which put you in a position to deliver your ideas better, faster, or cheaper than your competition. It's important to understand and explore these different types of capital as you organize your innovation effort. When you leverage your capital and acknowledge the capital you lack, you'll be positioned to make the most of your natural advantages and better understand your limitations. In other words, you'll be able to answer the question, "Why you?"

Human Capital

Each of us has a unique combination of skills, abilities, knowledge, and expertise. We acquire, expand, and improve this "human capital" toolkit through circumstances or innate interests over a lifetime. We often associate human capital with hard skills like the ability to engineer a machine, speak a second language, or code. Or we might think of them along traditional lines within a business, e.g., sales, marketing, finance, or management. But the complex layers of experience and understanding go way beyond these skill classes.

You know things that others don't because you've experienced the world in a way that is wholly unique to you. You can do things that others can't because you possess a combination of abilities that can't be duplicated. Whether learned through discovery, exposure, or experience, this gives each of us special advantages. When combined in a team, these assets form competitive advantages, particularly when bringing a new idea to life. But just as we have unique configurations of human capital, others do too. Knowing your strengths and limitations is fundamental to understanding what you're good at and where you'll either want to avoid competing or where you'll need help.

Financial (Economic) Capital
This form of capital is familiar to everyone, even if you call it by other names: money, equipment, inventory, intellectual property, data, land...the list goes on. Unlike human capital, which can't be exchanged, financial or economic capital is any asset that can be readily bought, sold, or bartered. It's not difficult to understand why innovators fixate on financial capital. Money buys labor, materials, and technology. Those lead to products and services. And products and services are sold for more money. Without access to those resources, innovation stops. While we all know this, innovators don't always fully understand the assumptions they're making about their ability to access financial capital. Time and again, I talk with entrepreneurs who are convinced that all they need is a solid business plan, and some investor will come along and *poof* give them money. However, that is so rarely true that it's nearly a myth. While it's possible to raise money from friends, family, and social organizations based solely on an idea, it's rare that professional investors — high net worth individuals, angel networks, or venture capitalists — will invest money based solely on a business plan and a pitch.

Serious investors always aim to reduce their risk and maximize their return. Even at the earliest stages of a new venture, they'll need evidence you are solving a meaningful problem, have a product that works, can deliver your product, and have customers who want to buy it. (In other words, everything the Value Proposition Matrix helps you define.)

As you'll quickly notice, it takes money to gather that evidence. If this looks like another chicken-or-egg problem, you are correct. This is one of the most devilish paradoxes in innovation; it takes money to get money. That is why it's fundamentally important to organize your financial capital. Sometimes that means gathering seed money from savings, taking out a loan, or recruiting friends and family as early investors. This also means gathering the other tangible assets you have, like equipment, patents, or land.

As with many of the topics I've touched on, entrepreneurial finance is a deep and complex subject unto itself. To get a full picture of the processes, considerations, and complexities of innovation investment, I recommend reading Brad Feld and Jason Mendelson's *Venture Deals*.

Social (Reputational) Capital

There is another form of capital, sometimes called social or reputational capital. My father once explained reputational capital to me by adding a twist on the old saying, "It's not what you know; it's who you know." He said, "It's not what you know, but it's not who you know either. *It's who knows you.*"

When others know you or know of you, it can be a powerful asset. An extreme form of this is fame. If you're well-known, your notoriety is an asset you can leverage to build a new business. For example, John Elway, a Hall of Fame quarterback with the Denver Broncos, built a string of car dealerships called John Elway Autos in the Denver area. When he retired from the NFL in 1997, he sold those dealerships for over $80 million — nearly double what he'd earned during his 16-year playing career. Stars use their social capital to this effect all the time. Just think about all the celebrity-backed tequila brands out there, from stars like George Clooney, Kendall Jenner, and Sammy Hagar.

While most of us can't claim to be famous, what others know about us can be a powerful asset (or, in some cases, a liability). For example, if you've published research papers on material science in respected journals, you would probably find eager partners if you were to start a company developing chemical coatings to protect fabrics. Similarly, as a respected attorney, you would likely be able to find supporters if you launched a startup to help other attorneys manage cases using software. However, if the lawyer and the scientist in these scenarios traded places, their chances of success would be lower (all else being equal) due to a lack of reputational capital in spaces outside their fields of expertise.

But technical expertise is only one example of reputational capital. If you plan to sell a product to a niche group of customers, having experience as a part of that niche and speaking to those needs with authority can be a huge asset. If you want to sell a product that helps inner-city schools improve student outcomes, you'd have a significant leg up if you spent time as a teacher or administrator in an inner-city school district.

One of the quantifiable forms of social capital is your credit score. Financial capital (loans, investment, etc.) is harder to come by if your credit score — your reputational capital as it relates to personal finance — isn't sound.

More examples of reputational capital include a history of past accomplishments, academic degrees, and professional certifications.

Ask yourself: what sorts of social capital put me in a position to bring my idea to life? Where am I strongest, and where am I lacking, given the product or service I'm trying to launch? While you don't have to have A-list fame or a Nobel Prize winner's authority, you should, at a minimum, have some notable social capital to leverage, among your early adopters, within your industry, or with key support partners.

If you find that you lack reputational capital, it's not too late to develop more. Spend time meeting your consumers. Share your ideas with those communities. Perhaps most efficiently, add people to your team who have established capital in the circles that matter most to your venture. Invest time working and building a stronger connection to that space and the people who make up its social fabric. While this might be a longer road, mistakenly overlooking the importance of social capital can stifle important paths to success and growth, paths that your competition will certainly look to leverage.

Organizational Capital
If you're trying to innovate within an existing organization or sell a product to one, it's also important to discuss organization capital. Akin to reputational capital, this asset extends beyond what people know about you and stretches into what you know about the inner workings of a business or institution. This includes understanding how decisions get made inside of an organization, who has the power to take action, what sorts of problems or opportunities motivate key players, and what direction an organization is headed.

Knowing who to call, what to say, and when is a *huge* advantage. Entrepreneurs who leave an organization to sell products or services to their former colleagues often rely on this form of capital. Likewise, without it, you may find yourself at a significant disadvantage. If, as a new joiner, you jump into an intrapreneurial effort and others in the company don't hop on board (even if that was your mandate), that could signify a lack of social capital on your part. Like all forms of intangible capital, it's hard to develop organizational capital without earning it.

If you're eager to get your idea or business off the ground, it's probably frustrating to feel like having the right capital — in all its forms—might hold you back from your goals. But keep a few things in mind: First, hard work and intense effort are often effective ways to build capital. While not always true, reputational and human capital, in particular, tend to be meritocratic. Second, time isn't necessarily a variable in capital development. Some capital accrues quickly when other factors come together. Finally, while all the forms of capital we've discussed can be formidable assets, none on their own determine success. As with any asset, the right application of capital at the right time is as critical — if not more so — than simply having a vast amount of capital in any form.

Activate your network
The next time you talk with a successful innovator, ask how important their connections were to their success. In my experience, almost universally, the answer will land somewhere between critical and "I couldn't have done it without them."

The power of a network is well-documented. A 2009 study by MIT found a direct correlation between the number of links in a person's social network and their success as an entrepreneur. In 2019, researchers found a positive correlation between the number of LinkedIn connections a founder has and the amount of investment capital they raise. Again and again, having a strong and varied network has been shown to give the well-connected a demonstrable edge.

A network — who you know, who knows you, and who *they* know — is the support structure that sustains any innovation effort. No project is an island, and innovation is no exception. Money, customers, suppliers, partners, experts, advice, advocates; they will all likely flow through and from the people in your network.

My friend and fellow professor at Case Western Reserve University, Michael Goldberg, is a master of activating his network, often on behalf of our students. Whether he's reaching out to notable authors or CEOs, Michael has an almost magical ability to get in touch with people. In part, because of this quality, his Massive Open Online Course (MOOC), "Beyond

Silicon Valley," is the most translated course on Coursera.

Here are three valuable lessons I've learned from him over the years:

1. ***The best app on your phone is your phone.*** Texts, emails, and social media have enabled us to dash off a note to just about anyone. It's tempting to imagine that the person on the other end of that note is ready and waiting to respond to us. It also feels less intrusive to reach out in a way that lets someone else respond at their leisure. Both are often true, which is what makes digital communication so ubiquitous. But in an ocean of pings, alerts, and tweets, a phone call somehow stands out. When Michael has a number, he uses it. You should too. It makes your connections more active and vibrant. It also says the subject on your mind matters, and so does the other person.

2. ***Invite others to share in the project with you.*** We all want to feel like we're contributing to something — that our thoughts, ideas, and actions have value. Likewise, there's something deeply gratifying about being invited into the inner circle of a project. Michael uses both principles by sharing his projects with his network. In his case, he'll informally invite them to his class to add their expertise to a conversation or (more formally) to lecture on a topic that relates to the course. He seeks lots of opinions from the thought leaders in his life about the courses and content he's developing, at times deftly enmeshing his favorite brains into the creation process as full-fledged partners. In my case, Michael asked me to help him think through a new approach to the business model development course he was teaching at Case Western Reserve University's Weatherhead School of Management. Six months later, I

was co-teaching the course with him. Sharing your project with your network takes a humble heart, an open mind, and the ability to carefully select the right partners. But if you can manage this balancing act, you can use it to supercharge your project.

3. *Help serendipity happen, and not just for yourself.* Michael spends more of his time than most people "networking," making connections between and among his contacts. While he certainly leverages his network to further his personal projects, often, he's connecting other people to advance what's important to them. This generates a lot of goodwill and creates a plethora of valuable connections between a diverse set of people. This energy isn't always highly targeted, say, by introducing a startup founder to an expert in their industry. It's also about introducing two people simply because they're like-minded, share interests, or "should know each other." Michael's first thought never seems to be, "How can this person help me?" it's always, who do I know that can help this person? Consequently, Michael has one of the most vibrant and engaged networks I've ever seen.

Recruit some advisors

The most successful innovators cultivate and maintain a special segment of their network as advisors. While it's worth welcoming thoughtful and experience-based advice from a broad range of perspectives, advisors include a specific class of people who know something about what you're trying to do (and who are willing to make a concerted effort to help you). Sometimes this relationship is formal, e.g., in the case of a Board of Directors, or it can be informal and welded together based on the project's path. Whatever form they take, these relationships should serve as a touchstone of advocates you can call on for guidance.

I generally classify advisors into two types: experts and customers.

Expert advisors have some technical skill or experience related to your project and are willing to use that knowledge to inform your efforts. Technical experts like engineers, designers, marketers, financiers, and lawyers can provide specialized guidance. Generalists, particularly experienced innovators, can offer broader insights based on their hard-earned know-how. While the latter tend to be particularly helpful in the earlier stages of the innovation journey, a healthy mixture of both is invaluable.

Finding expert advisors may include tapping into your already-established network, finding a local cohort of successful innovators, or, depending on your needs, reaching several steps beyond your immediate connections. Several entrepreneurial ecosystems across the US have built a web of academics, experienced entrepreneurs, industry partners, and support organizations. Use them as much as possible as you search for the right combination of advisors.

Using the Value Proposition Matrix as a guide can be a helpful framework for understanding what kinds of experts may offer the most value to your effort. If you're still *listening* to customers, consider recruiting experts in that industry or those who have bought or sold products like yours. If you are *building* prototypes, engineering and intellectual property expertise can be critical. If you are *organizing* your team, the advice of financiers, accountants, and lawyers can be invaluable. And if you are *selling* your product, business development, marketing, and retail experts make for excellent resources. In all these cases, experienced innovators can offer a wealth of guidance.

Of course, it's quite likely that all these steps will be on your mind as you build your business, and areas of expertise often overlap. As such, you'll want to build a broad base of support and engagement and over-invest in cultivating those relationships.

It's important to note that you'll want to choose advisors

who mesh well with your approach and see your vision but who are also willing to give you direct, candid advice. You don't want unmitigated encouragement, but you don't want a constant stream of discordant critique either. A healthy group of advisors combines candid counsel with a bought-in, problem-solving mindset.

Whomever you recruit, understand that the relationship you're building is a two-way street. Expert advisors often donate their time, and in return, they'll expect you to lead capably, engage them in the process, and work diligently to put their advice to good use.

In addition to cultivating a group of expert advisors, consider creating a similar group of customer advisors. To do this, look to early adopters who deeply feel the problem you are trying to solve and are engaged in finding a solution. These could be customers who have purchased early versions of your product or consumers who have been particularly eager to give you feedback about their experiences concerning your idea.

Finding these customer advisors isn't easy. **Look to recruit them throughout the process of exploring your value proposition. When you have a particularly fruitful interaction with an early or highly engaged customer, ask if they would be willing to provide feedback on future product iterations.** Follow-up with these advisors as you make changes and let them know when their feedback impacts your thinking. Ideally, over time, these customers become invaluable resources and, ultimately, champions. While creating this type of relationship takes time and will never look like a formal "Board" relationship, it can provide an invaluable channel into the needs and motivations of your customers. In return, these customers (and, hopefully, many more like them) benefit from helping to craft a better product for themselves.

There's a common myth about innovators; that they are young, idealistic industry outsiders who see the world from a fresh perspective, making them well-positioned to disrupt the status quo. This myth has been repeated and amplified by a small group of highly visible, highly successful tech founders like Steve Jobs at Apple, Larry Page and Sergey Brin at Google, and Mark Zuckerberg at Facebook. While these tech giants founded companies that perch at the top of the S&P 500 — and therefore, dominate our image of the "Founder" — they are exceptions to the rule.

According to a study by Ben Jones at Northwestern University's Kellogg School of Management and Pierre Azoulay at MIT's Sloan School of Management, **the average age of a successful startup founder is 45**. The reasons have far more to do with their assets than their idealism or youthful zeal. "Relative to founders with no relevant experience," Jones and Azoulay found, "those with at least three years of prior work experience in the same narrow industry as their startup were 85% more likely to launch a highly successful startup."

While it's romantic to imagine diving into a startup armed with passion and guts, evidence suggests that you're far more likely to fail without a deep understanding of your target industry. There is no exact mix of experience, financial resources, and connections that will make the ultimate difference. Still, it's clear that a combination of all these factors plays a fundamental role in every innovator's success. Understanding how to amplify your assets and overcome those you lack will put you on a sound path.

Chapter Six
Bringing it Together

Synopsis: In this chapter I'll share a case study that describes how one innovator used the Value Proposition Matrix to explore his key assumptions and build a winning value proposition.

6.1 Battle Toss

Recall Russell, the Founder of Battle Toss. He used the VPM to design and follow a careful vetting process for his key assumptions. His experience is a textbook example of assumption-based innovation that drives home how the model works in the real world. Let's walk through the steps he took, the adjustments he made, and the results he saw along the way.

First, he began by *listening* to potential customers. Remember that he initially thought his first customers would be college students. To test this hypothesis, Russell took his rough prototype to parks, bars, community barbecues, fraternity houses, football tailgates, and other places people played outdoor games, like beer pong and cornhole. He watched people play the game, carefully noting what worked as expected and what didn't. He also interviewed players, both before and after their experiences, to learn as much as possible about what attracted them to the game, what other games they played, what they enjoyed, and what they thought could be better about Battle Toss.

This listening cycle proved to be an information goldmine.

Russell learned players loved that the game was built out of wood and metal. Far from wishing it was plastic, players raved about the sturdy, handcrafted feel of the unit. Even more importantly, he discovered that adults over 30 responded more favorably than younger adults or children. That all ages could play and enjoy the game made it particularly appealing for parents of young children who wanted a game the entire family could enjoy. This segment also liked that the game stood out from the mountains of plastic toys that tend to pile up in playrooms. Russell also learned that consumers wanted an easy way to store the game. They suggested better folding features and hooks for hanging it on door frames.

From there, Russell began to *organize* the team and, working with engineers at MAGNET, to build an MVP. Armed with feedback from early testers, MAGNET used design software and rapid prototyping tools like laser cutters to produce a wooden version of Battle Toss. It was durable and playable, with folding features that would make it easier to ship in a flat package. It was also safe and sturdy. But — and this is important — it wasn't perfect. There were myriad things that could have been improved with more time and money. Russell could have used higher quality, more expensive wood. He could have spent more time and money giving the product a smoother, more refined finish. He could have ensured that the components fit together more precisely. He could have made it easier to ship. No, it wasn't perfect. But it was good enough to sell. It was the perfect Minimum Viable Product.

A MAGNET engineer working on the Battle Toss MVP (left) and Russell, with a unit in development (right)

With his MVP, Russell went about getting those crucial first *sales*. He started by acquiring battletoss.com and setting up a simple website where customers could place orders. Then he reached out to some of the most enthusiastic players from his listening efforts, letting them know that a limited number of beta units were available for purchase. He made several sales on his website right away. He also hosted Battle Toss tournaments at local bars, offering free entry and Battle Toss units to the winners. Hundreds of people signed up, and he made dozens of sales. Beyond marketing opportunities, these events were rich sources of consumer feedback, which Russell diligently collected. Russell also captured videos, pictures, and quotes from customers, improving his website.

Based on this early-adopter feedback, Russell and the MAGNET team reworked the second prototype. For one, some customers complained that the laser cut units smelled burned. One commenter noted that the game smelled "like a campfire." With the help of MAGNET's engineers, he designed a version that could be quickly cut using a water jet, eliminating the burnt smell. He also decided to change the netting material to improve the ball bouncing action, build a better mechanism for collecting balls, and improve the channel design to make it easier to see the balls stack throughout the game.

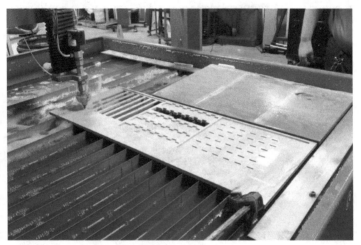

Battle Toss units being cut on a water jet in MAGNET's workshop

Battle Toss components

With another build cycle complete, Russell amped up his online sales efforts by listing Battle Toss on Amazon. He also *organized* his retail capabilities by adding an expert on Amazon sales to improve the product's visibility. Customers reacted with a mixture of enthusiasm for the concept and a desire for a better-built product. If you go to Amazon today, you'll see a few of the one- and two-star ratings, one of which says this:

 Amazon Customer

★★☆☆☆ **Wish I would have opened it before the return period expired**
Reviewed in the United States on April 25, 2019
Verified Purchase

Great concept, terrible quality! There are two L brackets that hold a piece of wood that is for the ball release. First off the L brackets are crooked and it looks like I let my kid put it together, second one of the L brackets was not drilled in the correct location and it prevents all of the balls in the section above from dropping. All of the clips that hold the box together for the balls at the bottom are made of wood and are very quick to fall apart including the two for the top of the box which is supposed to be removable. Once you put the box for the balls together at the bottom, the product no longer fits back in the box. The legs aren't very sturdy when you are putting it together/taking it apart. This is the first product that I have purchased on Amazon that I have REALLY wanted to return. Unfortunately I waited more then 30 days before we opened it on Easter and played with it for the first time. Don't make the same mistake!

If they ever come out with a better quality version I would be a buyer all day.

For many entrepreneurs, this feedback would be crushing. "Terrible quality." Ugh. "It looks like I let my kid put it together." Ouch. But Russell knew that this was an MVP. It wasn't designed to be perfect. It was designed to help him learn quickly. While other innovators might fixate on the negative, here's what we saw:

"Great concept … if they come out with a better quality version I would be a buyer all day."

Despite some serious disappointment with the product quality, this customer was still excited about what the product could be. Think about how much this customer must have loved the concept to say, "I would be a buyer all day (with improvements)" despite the initial "terrible quality" of the MVP. **This is what MVP feedback looks like. It's messy. It's harsh. But it's valuable.**

Inside each box, Russell had included a handwritten note thanking his customers and encouraging them to share their feedback. He responded quickly to negative feedback, including to the person who wrote the review above. He often provided new products or refunds to unhappy customers, shipping replacements around the country at no charge. But the orders continued to pour in, so much so that Russell exceeded his production capacity. With more orders than he could fill, he decided to sell exclusively through his website, his most profitable channel.

What Russell learned from that second round of sales further confirmed that the most enthusiastic early adopters were 30+ year-olds with families. When asked to estimate the product's retail price, this group often guessed a price that notably exceeded other consumer segments. As a result, Russell increased the price per unit and saw little change in the demand. This gave him the confidence to invest in another round of engineering improvements. Again working with MAGNET's engineers, he tweaked the product's design. He addressed the obvious issues pointed out by the unhappy Amazon customer and others, including the placement of some holes and the design on the ball box. In this new build phase, Russell also aimed to make the product more compact to decrease its shipping size. This led to a two-piece unit that the consumer could easily assemble themselves. Along the way, MAGNET's engineers further simplified the manufacturing process, cutting more than half the time needed to take the product from raw sheets of wood to boxed, ready-to-ship units. They also increased the quality of the wood and hardware and refined the fit and finish of the final product.

At this point, Russell also realized that he needed to again *organize* his efforts. Buoyed by the knowledge that his product had a viable market, Russell hired a law firm to help him address some questions from the United States Patent Office's Patent Examiner. He also engaged MAGNET's startup advisors and operations experts to help him build a more robust financial model and redesign his workshop to accommodate greater production volume.

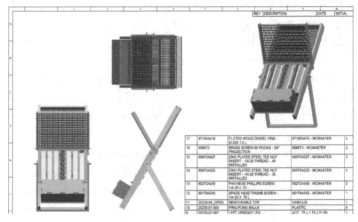

Concept drawings of the third Battle Toss MVP

Battle Toss players competing in a tournament held in Cleveland

Today, the demand for Battle Toss continues to exceed Russell's current capacity to make and ship units. His success has given Russell several options. He can grow by investing in manufacturing capability, license Battle Toss, or sell the company to a strategic buyer. With a patent on his product in hand and proven market demand, he can rest assured that his company is built on a solid strategic foundation. He understands his customer, the problem he's solving for them, what's unique about his solution, and the team he needs to deliver the product. He vetted his critical assumptions thoroughly and deliberately, allowing what he learned to inform his next steps. Recall that Russell initially believed his product should be made of plastic. Had he followed the traditional product development path based on that assumption, he may well have spent hundreds of thousands of dollars on tooling and equipment to build plastic products that consumers preferred in wood. Given what he learned along the way, he likely would've had to redesign the product, multiplying his production costs many times over. Instead, using the Value Proposition Matrix as his roadmap, he efficiently designed and launched a thriving business based on what his consumers truly wanted.

Chapter Seven
Biases

Synopsis: Human decision-making is fraught with biases. This has profound implications for innovators, who must make constant decisions while facing uncertainty. Understanding these built-in blind spots helps contextualize the common blunders innovators make and further underscores the crucial role assumptions play in innovation.

7.1

"Our comforting conviction that the world makes sense rests on a secure foundation: our almost unlimited ability to ignore our ignorance."

— Daniel Kahneman, Nobel Prize-winning Economist

The entrepreneur sitting across from me narrowed her eyes and, with utmost confidence, said, "Look, anyone who knows anything about this industry — and clearly you don't — knows that I'm going to be a millionaire." While this innovator was more direct than most, it wasn't the first time I had betrayed my ignorance or riled someone with my questions.

Innovators often have an overabundance of confidence and determination. Many don't appreciate probing questions, especially when those questions feel like uninformed skepticism. In this case, Jackie, the founder of a startup developing specialized pesticides, was expressing her frustration after I'd suggested some of her assumptions could use a bit more vetting. Specifically, I was asking for evidence to support or refute the guesses she had made about her target market and product. That didn't make Jackie very happy.

From her perspective, it's not hard to see why. She'd been working day and night on this project for years. She and her team had solved some very hard problems. She'd made impressive breakthroughs and felt she was developing something that could improve crop yields and, ultimately, feed more people. She'd even gotten some grant funding, attracted a few investors, and gathered a list of accomplished mentors. She wasn't bothered by her assumptions because she didn't think she was making very many. She knew a lot about this market. In her opinion, anything she didn't know was sure to be inconsequential. Whatever stood in her way was simply another obstacle she would face down to reach her goal. Besides, this didn't seem like an experiment to her. She was building a great product and giving it to the world. In my experience, there are countless innovators just like her.

Innovators don't see the world like everyone else. Where most of us see delay, inefficiency, expense, and irritation, innovators see opportunities for improvement through new solutions. That gift has pushed humanity toward brighter technological, cultural, political, and economic horizons for millennia. Innovators believe they can succeed where others have failed, see things to which others remain blind, and understand things that others haven't grasped. But embedded within that beautiful impulse to innovate can be a troublesome blind spot. Thus, while that belief sustains and drives innovators, it can also trap and fool them.

Sometimes innovators are simply wrong about the world. Customers aren't always as prevalent or eager as they appear. Problems that seem big and important to an innovator aren't always so important to consumers. Solutions, so compelling and elegant to a founder, fall flat with customers. Teams, seemingly capable and stable at the onset, don't live up to expectations or dissolve under the demands of a new venture.

In their confidence, innovators are prone to insist that the resistance they encounter is simply part of the innovation process — something to be surmounted, endured, or vanquished. As author and sales guru, Grant Cardone, puts it, "Until the world understands that you're not going away — that you are 100 percent committed and have complete and utter conviction and will persist in pursuing your project — you will not get the attention you need and the support you want." While it certainly takes commitment to innovate, innovators often confuse persistence with an unwavering commitment to one's own point of view.

An innovator's greatest strength is often their most glaring weakness. Confidence and grit beget both resilience and forward momentum, but they can also smother the ability to see and accept contradictory evidence and legitimate warning signs. To avoid that trap, it's critical to understand the universal human tendencies to overestimate the odds of success, avoid information that might prove us wrong, look for evidence to support what we think is true, and play countless other mental tricks on ourselves.

7.2 Your Baby is Ugly

I have three daughters, Tessa, Eloise, and Sadie. Here's what you need to know about these three little girls: they are the cutest children in the world. I just know it.

Other people agree with me too. Their grandparents and my wife certainly do. And it goes way beyond family. When my wife posts pictures of these kiddos, you wouldn't believe the likes she gets on Facebook and Instagram. When I show friends pictures on my phone, they gasp and coo and generally fall over themselves to tell me how adorable they are. Even my work colleagues ask to see new photos. They are the cutest children around, and it's not just me who thinks so.

Right? Not quite.

There's a common phrase — "telling someone their baby is ugly." It means delivering tough feedback about an emotionally charged or sensitive subject. That criticism can be about someone's work, idea, team, family, reputation — anything that's taken effort to cultivate, improve, or maintain. The phrase is used so often in business circles that much of the power has been drained from the metaphor. So, I've found it useful to start a conversation about biases and assumptions by bringing up my own babies and biases.

A business idea is a lot like a child. You conceive or adopt it, nurture it, protect it, guide it, invest in it, and hope it accomplishes great things.

When an innovator is talking about their idea, they're talking about the professional equivalent of a baby. They've spent a lot of emotional energy bringing it to life. They've staked their reputation and invested their savings on the attempt. Along the way, family, friends, and even colleagues have encouraged and supported their efforts. Every "Great idea!", "You can do it!" and "I believe in you!" lifts the innovator and pushes them through doubt and disappointments. Why not? Nobody wants to shoot down a hardworking, gutsy innovator. What good would it do to be negative? Innovation is hard enough. These support networks emerge the moment a business idea comes into the world, so they often grow emotionally connected to the project too.

All that energy and support serves a vital purpose. Parenthood is hard; arguably, the hardest job there is. Innovation is a close second.

Like a proud parent, an innovator can't help but believe that their idea is exceptional. They'll beat the odds. Their idea is smarter. It's going places. Emotions do that. They make it hard to see the object of your affection objectively.

The energy that carries both parents and innovators through the highs and the lows brings with it biases. Admitting these biases exist and that no one is immune to them is an important part of vetting any business concept. Harnessing them is the backbone of evidence-based innovation.

7.3 Innovation biases

As noted, behavioral economists and psychologists have recently begun to revolutionize our understanding of how people make decisions. Far from the classical microeconomic version of decision-makers, human beings are (to nobody's surprise) not always rational. Nor are we particularly good at assessing odds.

This research on inherent biases in human thinking, also called heuristics, was pioneered by two Israeli psychologists, Amos Tversky and Daniel Kahneman, the founding fathers on the subject. Kahneman and Tversky produced a prodigious body of knowledge, some of which eventually earned Kahneman the Nobel Prize in 2002. (Tversky tragically died in 1996 and Nobel Prizes are not awarded posthumously.)

Much of Kahneman and Tversky's work focused on the way the brain deals with decision-making under uncertainty. Because creating new products and services is fundamentally fraught with uncertainty, their work is highly relevant to the study and practice of entre- and intrapreneurship.

Creating a new business is littered with unknowns. As we've covered at length, the guesses innovators make about those unknowns can have an immense impact on their finances, families, and careers. In other words, starting a new company is a high-stakes gamble on your own abilities. When human beings gamble, we're especially susceptible to biases. What's more, when assessing our own skills, we are often deeply biased. I'll go over some well-studied heuristics and explore how each impact innovators. Some of the concepts below might look familiar, as I touched on many in previous chapters. Here, I've offered fuller detail.

Confirmation bias is the tendency to look for, recall, prioritize, and overvalue information that supports things we already believe to be true. This is one of the most persistent biases I encounter among innovators. The powerful urge to fixate on evidence that agrees with our ideas runs straight to the core of every entrepreneur's desires. Innovators believe they see things that the world does not, so everything that looks like it supports our guesses seems special, valuable, and uniquely useful.

I once had an entrepreneur report that 29% of survey respondents said they were interested in her product. When asked why 71% of people weren't interested, she confessed that she hadn't investigated that. "With almost 30% of people expressing interest, why concern myself with people who clearly didn't get it?" she asked. For her, positive survey responses were enough. Looking for more information among the disconfirming data became an afterthought.

Willfully ignoring the reasons someone wouldn't buy a product is a classic case of confirmation bias. While finding a niche, as we've discussed, is wise, innovators can find valuable clues about their product's viability by examining it through the eyes of its skeptics and detractors. Often, it's those who spot flaws who can most effectively articulate those shortcomings with the potential to sink a venture. While it's not crucial to satisfy these doubts in all cases (early adopters are, after all, usually willing to overlook some imperfections), an innovator should do their best to be aware of those limitations.

Worse still, innovators tend to shy away from tough feedback while actively seeking encouragement or praise. Knowing that they should "talk to a lot of people about their idea," they'll find receptive family, friends, and colleagues with whom to share the merits of their ideas. Their audience inevitably responds positively. What incentive do they have to be negative and crush an energetic innovator's dreams? "Sure, that's a great idea," these people will say. Unfortunately, this kind of feedback acts as a hallucinogenic for an innovator. It deceives them into believing that they've discovered something the market wants, rather than what they've really discovered, that people are prone to tell you what they think you want to hear. It's worth repeating, **succumbing to confirmation bias is one of the most common and dangerous mistakes early-stage innovators make.**

Anchoring is when we give greater weight to the information we encounter first. Anchoring also happens when we feel, experience, or notice information more intensely. When an innovator initially explains an idea to an audience, the impressions they gather (often positive) create a powerful anchor to that idea. Likewise, if an innovator feels a particular problem deeply, that intensity tends to inflate their estimate for how prevalent and potent that problem truly is.

Anchoring plagues innovators because the ideas that spark new businesses often come from compelling experiences and insights. Seized by the intoxicating feeling of having discovered a valuable idea, it's easy to stay fixed on a position and put undue weight on that first burst of innovation energy rather than logically assess the waves of evidence that follow. Examples of anchoring abound in innovation efforts. I worked with one innovator who expressed exasperation that nobody was willing to pay him what he thought his Minimum Viable Product was worth. His first prospective customer had said that she thought the price should be three times the original price. Virtually no one else agreed. Yet, anchored to the high price, this innovator stubbornly refused to discount the product.

Availability bias comes from the belief that what we see around us represents the wider world. This heuristic leads us to believe that what we know and see is common.

On the first day of business school, my Marketing professor asked us a question: "How many of you have a passport." Of the fifty or so students in the class, seemingly all of the hands rose. Now, she said, what percent of adults in the United States would you guess have a passport? "80 percent," someone called out. "75," another person offered. I remember thinking that both numbers seemed low. "Only 36 percent of Americans have a passport," she said flatly. "Never forget that you are weird. You do not represent the average person. In marketing, you never speak for your customers. Your peers don't either. Your customers speak for themselves, and their experiences and perspectives are unique and unrelated to yours."

This was an excellent example of Availability bias in action. The class, having seen a room full of hands go up, were primed to believe that the proportion around them approximated the average population of the United States. Everyone in this US business school classroom seemingly had a passport, so most Americans must have a passport. In fact, the available evidence led us to dramatically incorrect conclusions.

Availability commonly biases innovators in much the same way. What innovators see day-to-day leads to all sorts of incorrect assumptions.

While the family and friends who support our innovative efforts provide an invaluable support structure, well-meaning encouragement often reinforces the availability bias. "Everyone I know says they'd buy this," and "Everyone I've talked to has this problem." are common refrains rooted in availability bias. One entrepreneur developing a new bathroom fixture told me that he had yet to encounter anyone who wouldn't buy his product. Yet, when pressed, we eventually determined that his idea would only be useful in about 30% of US bathrooms. Not surprisingly, everyone he'd spoken with about the product up to that point knew him personally. Kahneman called this the "what-you-see-is-all-there-is" problem, and it bedevils entrepreneurs.

The Curse of Knowledge is a blind spot that occurs when we understand a subject so well that we can't see or appreciate the questions, doubts, and misunderstandings of lesser-informed people. We forget what it's like to discover and understand what we've come to know. To some degree, every innovator falls victim to this bias. Stuffed full of information, research, and technical understanding, innovators struggle to empathize with people encountering their product, idea, or insight for the first time. That leads innovators to over or under-communicate their ideas. Of course, failing to clearly explain the idea limits the quality of the evidence an innovator can gather about their product, market, or consumer.

Recency bias is the tendency to place greater emphasis on new information. Importantly, "new" doesn't necessarily mean up to date. It just means that we give more credit to whatever we've learned, seen, heard, or experienced lately. For example, it's easy for innovators to take a recent customer conversation and emphasize those insights in the next prototype, rather than giving equal weight to previous customer interviews.

The Overconfidence effect is when we believe our ideas have a better chance of succeeding than other ideas, given the same or similar starting conditions. In a gambling context, this shows up when a gambler believes they can beat the odds. Innovators are notorious for believing that they have a special skill, insight, ability, or passion that others do not. While that confidence alone can be a powerful asset, it can also be a liability. Overconfidence leads people to take unwise risks, disregard useful information, and ignore the voices of mentors and well-meaning skeptics.

Stereotyping is what cognitive psychologist, Steven Pinker, defines as "projecting the typical traits of a group on any individual that belongs to it." Stereotyping is commonly associated with race, ethnicity, gender, sexual orientation, and other characteristics that lead people to judge individuals based on the group to which they (ostensibly) belong.

Apart from the social ills that this creates, it's also a dangerous, albeit tempting, practice for innovators. Particularly when segmenting customers, innovators tend to believe that a point of evidence gathered from someone who represents part of a particular group, therefore, applies to all members of that group. I've seen this bias lurking in value proposition hypotheses many times. Whether it's a belief that all new moms have certain needs or that millennials have a common set of attitudes or traits, this bias easily seeps into our assumptions.

Each of these heuristics can wreak havoc for innovators, often combining and overlapping to further obscure the facts. Unfortunately, this short list represents only a portion of the biases that psychologists and behavioral economists have identified. These biases, and many others, lead to mistakes, both big and small because they keep founders from fully identifying and assessing their fundamental assumptions.

It's probably no coincidence that early thought leaders on assumption-based innovation, like Eric Ries and Steve Blank, began publishing right around the time Tversky and Kahneman's work on bias was coming to prominence. While the idea that human beings aren't always rational actors has been around since time immemorial, classical economic theory relies strongly on the belief — the assumption — that we are smart, self-interested, and, above all, rational. With that frame of reference, it's little wonder that innovators have had few tools with which to discuss (and perhaps even thwart) irrational decision-making. That is, until the advent of assumption-based innovation.

Chapter Eight
The Winding Road to Success

Synopsis: The entrepreneurial journey is never as straightforward as innovators hope. Even the most successful attempts at innovation encounter unforeseen challenges and intimidating obstacles. But mistakes, misses, and setbacks are part of the innovator's bargain. In return, innovators get to reap the personal (and sometimes financial) rewards that come from hard work and undaunted exploration. Often, the world is better off as a result.

8.1

"Ever tried. Ever failed. No matter. Try again. Fail again. Fail better."
— Samuel Beckett, Playwright and Novelist

I'm grateful for every innovator I've ever met. Each one has inspired, educated, or challenged me in a new way. Out of profound respect, I've aspired to challenge, inspire, and educate each one of them in return. Writing this book is part of that effort, a way to explain a system that (I hope) brings some clarity, direction, and order to a confusing, scary, and risky endeavor. But despite my sincerest efforts, I have yet to keep a single innovator from the bumps and bruises that are an inevitable side effect of innovation.

The path to commercial success simply isn't ever going to be a smooth, straight line that rises to the right, like this:

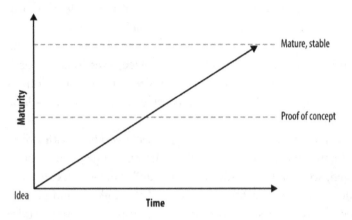

If your efforts don't look like a straight, upward climbing line, you should know that you aren't alone. A realistic picture of innovation looks more like peaks and valleys, rising, then falling, but always moving forward, always attempting to rise again.

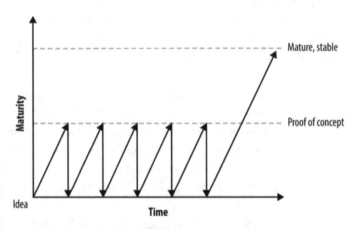

"You know that old saw about a plane flying from California to Hawaii being off course 99% of the time — but constantly correcting..." asked Evan Williams, co-founder of Twitter, "the same is true of successful startups, except they may start out heading toward Alaska."

This is a far more realistic picture of the modern innovation journey, despite vast popular mythology that suggests otherwise. We've all seen the magazine cover photos of successful entrepreneurs, standing tall, arms folded, eyes looking confidently into the camera, with their sleek Silicon Valley offices glistening in the background. Those pictures say it all — look at our success.

Following the same theme, the media floods us with stories of entrepreneurs who built their empires in one great inspired step, seemingly from idea to billion dollar buy-out. New products appear to mushroom on store shelves, glossy and perfected. High-flying startups tout their industry-disrupting service lines and brag about their nine-figure valuations.

But underneath that carefully crafted exterior of success sits the ruins of other failed ideas. The real stories are soaked to the bone with rejection and doubt. They rarely show what it's like to experience a buyer's rejection, an expensive marketing flop, a ruined shipment, a superior competitive product, a hacker's digital ransom note, an irate customer's review, an overdrawn bank account, or a cherished relationship cracking under the strain of risk and fear. This is what innovation really looks like.

Rightly or wrongly, this reality keeps a lot of bright people from building something potentially marvelous. Maybe that's because these innovators believe they need a "stroke of brilliance" and an idea good enough to vanquish any obstacle. Perhaps it's because they believe they lack the resources to launch the perfect idea in its scaled, polished form. Or maybe they simply don't know where to start.

All of these are essentially measuring the likelihood of success based on the quality and strength of the starting point. But, seen through the prism of assumption-based innovation, success looks like much smaller and more achievable steps. It can be assessed by the soundness and flexibility of the innovation plan. Success doesn't have to be measured in revenue. It can be measured by the innovator's ability to gather new information about their assumptions and adjust to it. In the words of Eric Ries, "Learning is the essential unit of progress."

The challenge, then, is not to come up with the perfect idea, gather all the right resources, and achieve instant scale, but to make a plan that is resilient and nimble enough to uncover the cracks and inconsistencies in an idea. The Value Proposition Matrix is meant to do just that.

No innovation framework is perfect, just like no business idea is perfect at conception. As much as I believe in the power of the VPM toolset, I also acknowledge the gulf between talking about these ideas and implementing them. Implementation is much, much harder. That means road-testing this approach probably won't feel as clean as the stories I've used to explain it. That can be said about any innovation toolset.

Launching an innovation is complicated. So, just as I recommend experimenting with a value hypothesis, I encourage innovators to think about this framework as an experimental process in itself. I suggest, first, trying to answer the core value questions and identifying one assumption that seems the most pressing. Run one simple experiment, then revisit the value proposition matrix. Adjust quickly to fit the learnings and the unique situation. The simpler the starting point, the more likely an innovator will find a useful insight using these tools.

It takes time and patience to use the VPM, but that's typically not where I see people struggle. **When experimental innovation stalls, it usually does so because innovators engage customers too late in the process, then ignore or refute unwelcome feedback.** That behavior, I believe, stems from a deep-seated aversion to failure. Nobody likes to be wrong, rejected, or criticized, particularly on something as personal, expensive, and consequential as building a new business. It's much more tempting to keep innovation efforts protected from the unforgiving eye of the market. As we've discussed, the best innovators do just the opposite. The market sharpens new ideas in a way that no amount of planning, development, or research can.

To armor themselves against inevitably tough market feedback, innovators should treat every effort like an experiment. Turn beliefs into hypotheses and label them that way. If progress is learning rather than being right, the stomach-churning twists and turns of innovation will feel like opportunities rather than threats.

There are rewards for the wise innovator. Certainly, there may be a financial upside when a product finds an enthusiastic market. But an experimental approach should also blunt the downside risk in faulty ideas, limiting the amount of time and money an innovator might spend building something the market doesn't want. Spending the minimum amount of time and money to learn as much as possible about the most important aspects of an idea — the critical assumptions — is the shortest path to better outcomes and less costly mistakes.

Beyond better outcomes, an innovator with grit earns a place among those intrepid visionaries who make the world a better place. Virtually every product in our lives, from vaccines and semiconductors to soda cans and cell phones, was once an idea in the mind of a brave, persistent innovator. To join those ranks, in any fashion, is to take up the call that has driven civilization forward.

If this is your path, then focus on the most important questions. Experiment, get customers, make them happy, grow, and of course, never lose sight of your critical assumptions.

Appendix

Figure A — The Four VPM Questions

Customer   Team

| Who will be your first customer? | What special assets does your team have? |
| What problem are you solving? | What unique product are you offering? |

Problem   Solution

Figure B — The Four VPM Questions + Assumptions

Figure C — The VPM, divided into demand and supply questions

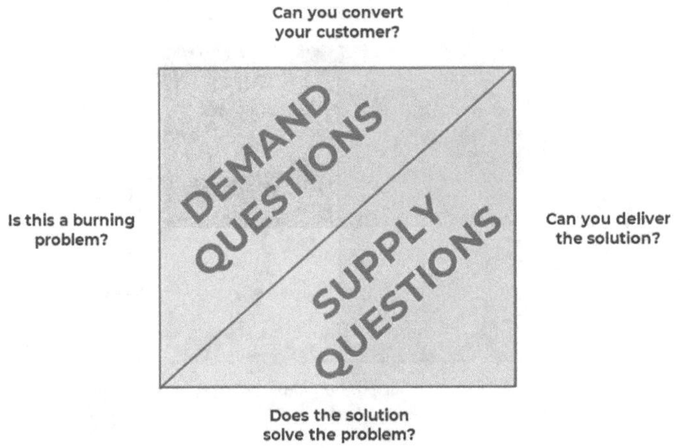

Can you convert
your customer?

DEMAND
QUESTIONS

SUPPLY
QUESTIONS

Is this a burning
problem?

Can you deliver
the solution?

Does the solution
solve the problem?

Figure D - The VPM + Vetting Activities

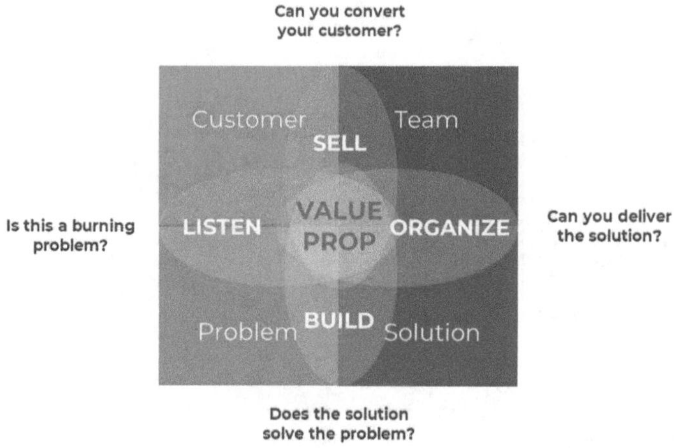

Figure E — The VPM vetting activities checklist

Listening

- Experience
- Observation
- Research
- Surveys
- Interviews

Selling

- Ad response
- Information exchange
- Joint development agreements
- Pre-orders
- Try-and-buy
- Sales

Building

- Benchmarking
- Prototyping
- Controlled testing
- Field testing

Organizing

- Competitive scouting
- DTR (Define the Relationship)
- P&L Sketch
- Key sources of capital
- IP landscape assessment
- Advisors

Endnotes

I use many sources in this book, including scores of books, articles, websites, interviews, and my personal experience working with startup founders, corporate innovators, executives, consultants, lawyers, engineers, students, educators, and investors. I have chosen to cite only those sources that I mention directly, from which I use specific data, or that I quote verbatim.

All image credits are referenced in the chapter notes in the order in which they appear.

Unless otherwise stated, the viewpoints in this book are my own and based on my own research and experiences and are not the viewpoints of any individual or organization in this book, including MAGNET: The Manufacturing & Growth Advocacy Network and Case Western Reserve University.

Notes to Preface

I use the term "innovator" a lot throughout this book. While words like innovation and innovative are used widely today, attempting to define innovation itself has sparked many a heated argument. At the risk of toppling headlong into that debate, I frequently refer to "innovators" for simple expediency. While I acknowledge that there are many types of innovators, here I use the term to mean anyone who is in the process of developing or exploring a new business value proposition. If that's not you but you still consider yourself an innovator, please forgive me. I've simply chosen to use the term to cover a broad range of entrepreneurs, founders, co-founders, corporate leaders, product developers, and intrapreneurs. Thank you for indulging my shorthand.

The quote from Ben Horwitz comes from Freischlad, Nadine, et al. "Ben Horowitz dropped some wisdom at Tech in Asia Tokyo 2015." Tech in Asia, 10 September 2015, https://www.techinasia.com/ben-horowitz-tech-in-asia-tokyo-2015. Accessed 24 November 2021.

Notes to Chapter One

I make several references to Lean Innovation ideas, particularly in this chapter. I have cited several such authors who have greatly influenced my thinking. They include:

Blank, Steve, and Bob Dorf. The Startup Owner's Manual: The Step-By-Step Guide for Building a Great Company. Wiley, 2020.

Constable, Giff, and Frank Rimalovski. Talking to Humans: Success Starts with Understanding Your Customers. Giff Constable, 2014.

Kowitz, Braden, et al. Sprint: How to Solve Big Problems and Test New Ideas in Just Five Days. Simon & Schuster, 2016.

Pigneur, Yves, et al. Business Model Generation: A Handbook for Visionaries, Game Changers, and Challengers. Edited by Yves Pigneur and Tim Clark, Wiley, 2010.

Ries, Eric. The Lean Startup: How Today's Entrepreneurs Use Continuous Innovation to Create Radically Successful Businesses. Crown Business, 2011.

Smith, Alan, et al. Value Proposition Design: How to Create Products and Services Customers Want. Wiley, 2015.

Information about Marriott's innovation efforts come from bizjournal.com, "Marriott Gets Hip", Accessed December 21, 2021, and theguardian.com, "The Pop-ups That Made Hotel Revenues Go Sky High", Accessed December 21, 2021.

Information about Google Ventures innovation process comes from Kowitz, Braden, et al. Sprint: How to Solve Big Problems and Test New Ideas in Just Five Days. Simon & Schuster, 2016.

Information about Lego's Futures Lab comes from fastcompany.com, "How Lego Became the Apple of Toys", Accessed December 21, 2021.

Information about the Department of Defense's Hacking for Defense program comes from h4d.us

The statistics about why startups fail are from CB Insights Research, "Top 12 Reasons Startups Fail", "https://www.cbinsights.com/research/startup-failure-reasons-top/. Accessed December 1, 2021

Information about Performance Indicator comes from Corts, Kenneth S. "Performance Indicator." Harvard Business School Case 702-480, May 2002. (Revised May 2003.)

The Lean Canvas comes from Maurya, Ash. Running Lean: Iterate from Plan A to a Plan That Works. O'Reilly Media, Incorporated, 2012.

The quote by Joseph Schumpeter comes from Schumpeter, Joseph A. Capitalism, socialism and democracy. HarperCollins, 1975.

The story about Dry Goods comes from my own experience and as captured in the case by Shein, J.B., Joyce, T. and Cornuke, B. (2017), "Dry Goods", Kellogg School of Management Cases. https://doi.org/10.1108/case.kellogg.2016.000103

Image 1 was created by Brandon Cornuke

Image 2, the Business Model Canvas, was released under Creative Commons license and is open for building other approaches and variations on the concept courtesy of Strategyzer.com. It was modified with section labels by Brandon Cornuke.

Notes to Chapter Two

I use the term "Product" in the Value Proposition Matrix framework and throughout this book. For the sake of brevity, I intend the term to encompass any good - be it physical or digital - or service imagined, created, or delivered by an innovator.

The quote by E.E. Comings comes from Commings, E E. Collected Poems. vol. 1, New York: Harcourt, Brace and Co., 1938.

The concepts about early adopters and the adoption curve come from Marshall, Larry R., and Everett M. Rogers. Diffusion of innovations. Free Press, 2003.

Information about personal computers in US households comes from the US Census Bureau, https://www2.census.gov/programs-surveys/demo/tables/computer-internet/1984/p23-155/tab05.pdf, Accessed December 21, 2021.

The quote by Clayton Christensen is from Christensen, Clayton. The Innovator's Dilemma. Harper Business, 2011.

Credit for the method of narrowing a target by asking three questions goes to Julie Hennessy, Clinical Professor of Marketing at Northwestern University's Kellogg School of Management.

Statistics on the number of mothers in the US comes from the US Census Bureau, https://www2.census.gov/programs-surveys/demo/tables/families/2020/cps-2020/taba3.xls, Accessed December 21, 2021.

Information about the Toyota Production System and the Five Whys comes from Wikipedia.org, https://en.wikipedia.org/wiki/Five_whys#cite_note-5, Accessed December 21, 2021.

Information about organic farming in the United States comes from the USDA, https://www.usda.gov/media/blog/2020/10/28/organic-thriving-agriculture-segment. Accessed December 21, 2021.

Information on Miller Lite's advertising history comes from Wikipedia.org, https://en.wikipedia.org/wiki/Miller_Lite, Accessed December 21, 2021.

The concepts and associated quotes about cognitive biases come from and are informed by Kahneman, Daniel. Thinking, Fast and Slow. Farrar, Straus and Giroux, 2011.

The Dollar Shave Club video I reference comes from Dubin, Michael, and Lucia Aniello. "DollarShaveClub.com - Our Blades Are F***ing Great." YouTube, 6 March 2012, https://www.youtube.com/watch?v=ZUG9qYTJMsI. Accessed 24 November 2021.

Information about Gillette's pricing strategy comes from the Wall Street Journal, https://www.wsj.com/articles/gillette-bleeding-market-share-cuts-prices-of-razors-1491303601. Accessed December 21, 2021.

Image 1 was found on https://commons.wikimedia.org/w/index.php?curid=18525407 from Rogers, E. (1962) Diffusion of innovations. Free Press, London, NY, USA., Public Domain.

Notes to Chapter Three

The quote by Donald Rumsfeld comes from Defense.gov News Transcript: DoD News Briefing – Secretary Rumsfeld and Gen. Myers, United States Department of Defense (defense.gov)". February 12, 2002. Archived from the original on March 20, 2018.

The story about True Fit comes from a classroom interview with Bill Adler conducted at Case Western Reserve University by Brandon Cornuke and Michael Goldberg on November 18, 2019

Image 1 was created by MAGNET: The Manufacturing Advocacy and Growth Network

Notes to Chapter Four

Parts of this chapter relied on Constable, Giff, and Frank Rimalovski. Talking to Humans: Success Starts with Understanding Your Customers. Giff Constable, 2014.

The Instacart story was found, in part, on Forbes.com, https://www.forbes.com/sites/jenniferwang/2020/06/17/instacart-founder-apoorva-mehta-becomes-a-billionaire/?sh=7bdf1b077e02. Accessed December 21, 2021.

Information about the differences between intent and action comes from:

LaPiere, Richard T. (1934). "Attitudes vs. Actions". Social Forces. 13 (2): 230–237. doi:10.2307/2570339. JSTOR 2570339

Sheeran, P. (2002). Intention-behaviour relations: A conceptual and empirical review. European Review of Social Psychology, 12, 1-36.

Schmidt, J., Bijmolt, T.H.A. Accurately measuring willingness to pay for consumer goods: a meta-analysis of the hypothetical bias. J. of the Acad. Mark. Sci. 48, 499–518 (2020). https://doi.org/10.1007/s11747-019-00666-6

The quote by Jeff Glueck comes from a classroom interview conducted by Brandon Cornuke at Case Western Reserve University on October 26, 2020

Information about Dropbox comes from TechCrunch.com, https://techcrunch.com/2011/10/19/dropbox-minimal-viable-product/. Accessed December 21, 2021.

The quote by Sun Tzu comes from Sunzi, and Wu Sun. The Art of War. Translated by Thomas F. Cleary, Shambhala, 1988.

The story about William Bradford's 1704 print advertisement comes from "Collections Online: The Boston Newsletter, number 1." Massachusetts Historical Society, https://www.masshist.org/database/186. Accessed 24 November 2021.

The definition of "vetting" comes from the Oxford Advanced Learner's Dictionary at OxfordLearnersDictionaries.com." Oxford Learner's Dictionaries, https://www.oxfordlearnersdictionaries.com/us/definition/english/vetting. Accessed 24 November 2021.

The quote by Mike Tyson can be found in 1987 August 19, Oroville Mercury-Register, Biggs has plans for Tyson (Associated Press) as cited by Quoteinvestigator.com https://quoteinvestigator.com/2021/08/25/plans-hit/. Accessed December 23, 2021.

The post about problems with horseflies was found on Reddit.com

Notes to Chapter Five

The quote by Sir James Dyson comes from "Failure Doesn't Suck." Fast Company, 1 May 2007, https://www.fastcompany.com/59549/failure-doesnt-suck. Accessed 1 January 2022.

The quote by Steve Jobs comes from a 2003 60 Minutes interview, which can be found at https://www.youtube.com/watch?app=desktop&v=ZUfzXz23ndo. Accessed 1 January 2022.

Statistics about intellectual property litigation in the United States comes from Huang, Henry Y. "2020 in review: Patent litigation increases." White & Case LLP, 9 March 2021, https://www.whitecase.com/publications/article/2020-review-patent-litigation-increases. Accessed 24 November 2021.

For additional information on innovation investing see Feld, Brad and Jason Mendelson, Venture Deals: Be Smarter Than Your Lawyer and Venture Capitalist. Hoboken, N.J.: Wiley, 2013

Information about the sale of John Elway Autos comes from "Elway Sells Car Dealership to Huizenga." The Washington Post, 29 October 1997, https://www.washingtonpost.com/archive/sports/1997/10/29/elway-sells-car-dealerships-to-huizenga/c048c1ff-b5fa-4189-b724-ff65c49a8967/. Accessed 24 November 2021.

Information about the correlation between the number of links in a person's social network and their success as an entrepreneur comes from "The Power of Alumni Networks - Success of Startup Companies Correlates With Online Social Network Structure of Its Founders." DSpace@MIT, https://dspace.mit.edu/handle/1721.1/66586. Accessed 24 November 2021.

Information about the correlation between the number of LinkedIn connections a founder has and the amount of investment capital they raise comes from Banerji, Devika, and Torsten Reimer. "Startup founders and their LinkedIn connections: Are well-connected entrepreneurs more successful?" Computers in Human Behavior, vol. Volume 90, no. 1, 2019, Pages 46-52. https://www.sciencedirect.com/, https://www.sciencedirect.com/science/article/abs/pii/S0747563218304084.

Statistics about the average age of successful startup founders comes from "Research: The Average Age of a Successful Startup Founder Is 45." Harvard Business Review, 11 July 2018, https://hbr.org/2018/07/research-the-average-age-of-a-successful-startup-founder-is-45. Accessed 24 November 2021.

Notes to Chapter Six

Information about Russell Horner's patent can be found at Horner, Russell J., inventor. Apparatus for playing a game and method. 3 Dec. 2019. U.S. Patent 10493343B2. Google Patents, www.google.com/patent/US10493343B2/. Accessed 24 Nov. 2021.

Image 1 was taken by Brandon Cornuke

Images 2-4 were taken by Rahul Narian

Image 5 was found on Amazon.com

Image 6 was created by MAGNET: The Manufacturing Advocacy and Growth Network

Image 7 was taken by Crystal Madrilejos/Tenlo (tenlo.com)

Notes to Chapter Seven

There is a vast body of knowledge available on cognitive biases. While I reference the work of Daniel Kahneman and Amos Tversky extensively, a growing list of cognitive biases and citations can be found at https://en.wikipedia.org/wiki/List_of_cognitive_biases.

The quote by Daniel Kahneman is from Kahneman, Daniel. Thinking, Fast and Slow. Farrar, Straus and Giroux, 2011.

The quote by Grant Cardone is from Cardone, Grant. The 10x Rule: The Only Difference Between Success and Failure. Hoboken, N.J.: Wiley, 2011.

Information about the percent of Americans with valid passports was found at YouGov, https://today.yougov.com/topics/travel/articles-reports/2021/04/21/only-one-third-americans-have-valid-us-passport. Accessed December 23, 2021.

The quote by Steven Pinker is from Pinker, Steve. Enlightenment Now: The Case for Reason, Science, Humanism, and Progress. New York: Penguin Books, 2018.

Notes to Chapter Eight

The quote by Samuel Beckett is from Beckett, Samuel. Westward Ho. Riverrun Press, Inc, 1990.

The quote by Evan Williams was referenced by Brikman, Jim. "A Minimum Viable Product Is Not a Product, It's a Process: Building Product, Experimentation, MVP." Y Combinator, https://www.ycombinator.com/library/4Q-a-minimum-viable-product-is-not-a-product-it-s-a-process. Accessed 25 November 2021.

The quote by Eric Ries is from Ries, Eric. The Lean Startup: How Today's Entrepreneurs Use Continuous Innovation to Create Radically Successful Businesses. Crown Business, 2011.

Acknowledgements

There are simply not enough words to describe how grateful I am to the many loving, generous, remarkable people who helped me with this book. However, I would like to offer special thanks to:

My wife, Whitney Cornuke, for being my fiercest ally, my safe harbor, and biggest fan; My mother, Sherre Ritenour, for showing me what it means to be brave and for never once letting me forget that I have value; My father, Bob Cornuke, for teaching me to question the world's assumptions and to embrace every adventure; Nate Reyher, my brother and consigliere; Tim Joyce, my first and best co-founder; Michael Goldberg, for giving me an opportunity to teach bright minds, a platform to share my ideas, and open access to your boundless network

My incredible colleagues at MAGNET, who have supported, inspired, and labored alongside me to apply and refine these ideas hundreds of times over. Thank you for giving me your trust, and for relentlessly serving our clients and our community; and a special thank-you to Ethan Karp, for trusting me to use these tools in the real world, and for believing in me and this project with all your heart; and to Alec Simon, for working tirelessly to sharpen these ideas and share them with our clients and students.

My readers and advisors, including John Brandt, Allen Brenner, Doug Degirolamo, Sarah Deutsch, Ian Drummond, Amy Hess, Joe Jankowski, Joe Keithley, Carla Macklin, Mary Beth Marks, Christopher Mazziotto, Tiffany McNamara, Rahul Narain, Andrea Navratil, Phil Peron, Justin Plummer, David Sylvan, Jeff Sinclair, and Amy Young.

MAGNET, the National Institute of Standards and Technology, the National Manufacturing Extension Partnership Network, the Ohio Manufacturing Extension Partnership, and the Economic Development Administration for their generous support of this project.

My editor, Tria Tedford, for patiently and skillfully working my words and thoughts into something coherent, and for (even more) patiently waiting for me to finally let this project take flight.

And the many friends, students, clients, and colleagues who have lovingly endured the long process of conceiving, developing, and refining these tools, and those who encouraged me (sometimes with a loving but firm push) to write this book.

Photo by Katie Montague Malone

Brandon Cornuke has dedicated his career to helping innovators turn their ideas into growing businesses. He is a speaker, writer, educator, and entrepreneur. He has co-founded a consumer products company, served as consultant to hundreds of startups, and led transformation and innovation efforts inside multi-billion-dollar businesses. He has shared his innovation methodologies with some of the most respected organizations in the world, including Fortune 500 companies, major hospital systems, world-class cultural institutions, top universities, and professional sports teams. Brandon is the Vice President of Strategy & Innovation at MAGNET, Northeast Ohio's premier non-profit provider of manufacturing expertise, and teaches as an Adjunct Professor of Design & Innovation at Case Western Reserve University's Weatherhead School of Management. He holds an MBA from Northwestern University's Kellogg School of Management and lives with his wife and three daughters in Shaker Heights, Ohio.